Wax on Crafts

15
Decorative Techniques for Transforming Your Crafts

Miriam Joy

Schiffer Publishing Ltd

4880 Lower Valley Road • Atglen, PA 19310

Other Schiffer Books by the Author
Miriam Joy's Wax Design Techniques
ISBN: 978-0-7643-4467-1

Wax on Crafts Holiday Projects
ISBN: 978-0-7643-4955-3

Other Schiffer Books on Related Subjects
Decorating Eggs: Exquisite Designs with Wax & Dye, Jane Pollak,
ISBN: 978-0-7643-4654-5

● ●

Published by Schiffer Publishing, Ltd.
4880 Lower Valley Road
Atglen, PA 19310
Phone: (610) 593-1777; Fax: (610) 593-2002
E-mail: Info@schifferbooks.com
Web: www.schifferbooks.com

Library of Congress Control Number: 2015958033

Designed by RoS
Cover design by Justin Watkinson
Type set in Bellota/Candara
ISBN: 978-0-7643-5021-4

Printed in China

● ●

For our complete selection of fine books on this and related subjects, please visit our website at www.schifferbooks.com. You may also write for a free catalog.

Schiffer Publishing's titles are available at special discounts for bulk purchases for sales promotions or premiums. Special editions, including personalized covers, corporate imprints, and excerpts, can be created in large quantities for special needs. For more information, contact the publisher.

We are always looking for people to write books on new and related subjects. If you have an idea for a book, please contact us at proposals@schifferbooks.com.

● ●

Dedication

When I think back on my childhood there are two special people who stand out: my Aunt Jo Marie and my Uncle Sammy. These are the two most unselfish people I have ever known. Growing up on the Navajo reservation in Arizona was not always easy. The culture was so different and I did not always fit in. My parents were also busy with their lives. My father taught school on the weekdays and tried to manage and run a business in Colorado. So almost every weekend of my young life I would be in a van traveling eight hours over the Rockies to Montrose, Colorado. My parents left us (my four older sisters and me) at our aunt and uncle's house so we could play with our cousins and they could get their work done. Now, my aunt and uncle were very hard-working farmers. I cannot imagine how tired they were, but they always got up every Saturday morning around 1:00 to welcome us into their home. They never complained or made us feel unwelcome. Tucked us back in bed and talked to my parents for an hour or two, before going back to bed themselves, to get up and feed the cows in just a few hours.

They tried to give us a normal life during that time. I loved to ride horses with my cousin and feed the lambs for her 4-H projects. In the summer my cousin Joleen and I would walk to the waterfall or tube down the canal. On a real lazy day we would go fishing at the fishing hole but we usually ended up swimming instead. One of the biggest thrills for me was watching TV. We did not have one at home. My cousins and I would sometimes stay up all night Friday night so we could make sure we were awake for Saturday morning cartoons. Most of the time, sleep won!

My aunt always encouraged our artistic talents.
I cannot tell you how many bunches of weeds I would pick.
I would paint the weeds to color them and I'd put them into a vase
to give to my aunt.

They loved us unconditionally just like we were their own.
They fed us and never said a word about us being a burden.
But most importantly they would take us to Sunday school and church every Sunday.
They taught us the love of our Lord and how important he was in our lives.
It was here that I felt loved and belonged.

It still makes me cry just writing this dedication.
I love you guys and because of your love and support when life was crazy,
we turned out okay.
I still long for Colorado and the sight of your smiling faces.

Acknowledgments

I cannot start a book without first acknowledging the Lord Jesus Christ and all the ways He has blessed me. It is because of His love and blessings that any of this is possible. I thank Him for allowing me to shine His light in my little corner of the art world, and for bestowing on me the gift of art that has so richly blessed my life.

To the most wonderful husband in the world, I could not be Miriam Joy without my Buddy Boy. How can I begin to express my love and appreciation for all you do? You are the support crew that keeps me going. I struggle to find the words to express all that you do for me, both as an artist and businesswoman, but most importantly as my partner. You make me feel like the most loved woman in the world. I love our long walks and our heartwarming talks. Sitting with you in the swing with your arms around me and falling asleep at night in your arms. Thank you for being my husband and my best friend. I love you so much.

It takes a village to run Miriamjoy.com and, trust me, I could not do it without my village. From the people who believed in us and do our manufacturing to our very special friends who help out with products, you are wonderful people. Thank you for all you have done. For all the people who have helped us along the way, friends and family who have prayed for my business, special people who helped edit my books— you guys are the best village a girl could have.

To our children: each one of you has helped in your own special way. You believed in me and have helped me out so much. I cannot thank you enough for your love and support.

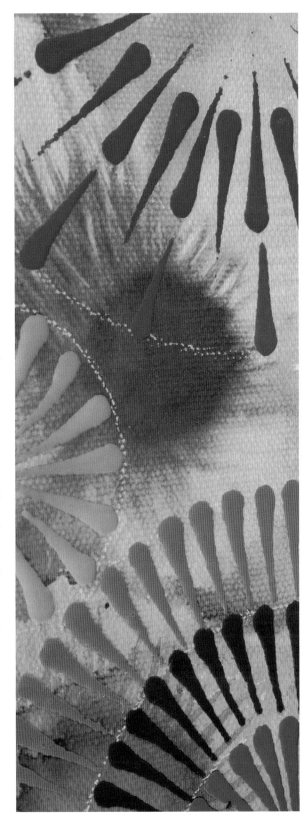

Add a little "*Joy*" to your life!

Contents

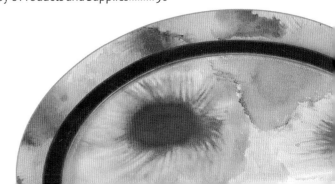

Introduction

This book is about color. Life is always about color. Since I was a little girl it has been about color. What was more colorful than a big box of crayons? I could not wait for school to start so I could get a fresh box of crayons, so many colors. Every color you could imagine.

My third grade teacher, Mrs. Copenbarger, who was a work of art herself, was very stylish for an older woman at that time. She wore purple dresses with purple go-go boots. Mrs. Copenbarger would give us wonderful coloring pages for the holidays. I could hardly wait for the next holiday so we could get a new picture to color. The color transformed the pages into art. And what do I use today for my art? Crayons! One of the most colorful forms of art I know. Come create with me. Start with color and apply it to other items, and add a little color to your life.

Growing up on the Navajo reservation, our only store was a trading post. With the nearest town being a hundred miles away, if you wanted something you learned how to make it. I guess that is how it all started. I made colorful bright flower arrangements out of ugly old weeds, and the vase was an empty plastic container wrapped with colorful yarn or string. I used anything nature was willing to provide.

Come with me and let's learn how to turn ordinary items into extraordinary pieces of art. Things that we take for granted around us every day, items that you might throw away without giving a second thought. Crafts do not have to cost a lot. I love to look for new craft items at my local dollar store, thrift store, or recycle store. And of course I have to go to our favorite craft store, where I check out all the dollar bins.

··· Warnings and Precautions ···

As with any crafting project, it's important to understand the warnings and precautions as you move through the steps of colorful creation. Note the following:

❶ MJ Low Temp Melting Pot, MJ Wax Design Tools, Embossing Tool, and the MJ Texture Brush Insert can all get very HOT. Use caution and do not touch the hot metal when using or handling these items. Be careful touching items heated with these tools. **They can become very HOT.**

❷ Always have adult supervision in cases where children are using the wax design process. Safety allows fun for everyone! Wax design is not recommended for children under eight years of age.

❸ The MJ Melting pot is an electrical device—caution should be used while using any electrical device.

❹ Use caution when working with a hobby knife: if a tool can cut through a crayon, it can cut you, too!

❺ Unplug the melting pot when not in use. **Do not leave the melting pot unattended!**

Chapter 1

Tools and Supplies

Using Crayola Crayons as Wax

For my wax I use Crayola crayons. Don't you love Crayola crayons? The smell brings back wonderful memories to the old and young alike. But seriously, where else can you find all of these colors in one box? And when you start to mix and match all the colors, it becomes unlimited.

Other waxes can be thin and require you to add color, so why not use crayons? It does make a difference for you to use Crayola brand crayons, though. They are brighter, thicker, and the color does not fade. At back-to-school time, you cannot beat the price of a box of twenty-four crayons—my favorite box. It has all the basic colors that I use the most and, as I said, is very cost-effective.

One of the things people are most amazed by is that each color works a little differently. The lighter colors, like yellow and yellow-greens, are thinner in consistency. It is not that you are doing anything wrong as you melt the crayon. The darker colors are a little thicker. Of course, there is one in every bunch that has to make its own rules, and for the Crayola crayons, it is white. The white crayon thinks it is a thicker color and goes on thicker, but can also act like a thinner color and can drip a little more.

When you are working with crayons, the tip of the crayon is the color the wax is going to be. Do not expect your color to come out the color of the label surrounding the crayon. A lot of the darker colors, such as blue or purple, look black when applied as wax. Make the color lighter by adding a sliver of white, until you get the desired color.

Treat your crayons just like paints. Mix and match them in the same way. For example, blue, green, and white mixed in equal amounts makes a beautiful turquoise color.

Of course the bigger boxes of crayons have a bigger variety of colors. You start to see gold, silver, bronze, and copper crayons. Just keep in mind that if you are doing a bigger project, you may need a couple crayons of the same color. (Colors like inchworm and mac and cheese are among my favorites.) The Crayola Gel FX crayons have bright and vivid colors.

Note: Read through the varied project instructions I've included for you here in their entirety before beginning. Then, if there is a video, though you do not need to view it to work on or complete your project, sometimes it's fun to see the design come together before digging in!

Have fun!

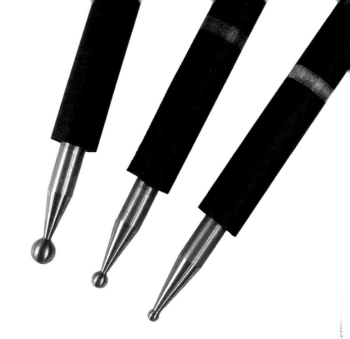

There are boxes of metallic and glitter crayons available, too. The metallic crayons have that metallic shine and can add so much to designs or Christmas ornaments. The glitter crayons contain glitter to give projects that extra sparkle. Just remember when using these colors, they add the sparkle and shine, but not the brightness that the regular crayons bring.

Do not be afraid to use old crayons. They do not go bad. Broken, worn, or discarded, they still work great. The end of a school year when kids are throwing away the worn-down or broken crayons and Sunday school programs can be among some of the best places to get unwanted crayons. Also, white is not a favorite color, so it may be easy to come by!

··· About MJ Wax Tools ···

The Miriam Joy Product line was created by dreaming. I started playing with wax and realized how amazing it was. I knew that there were so many ways to use it, but I needed tools that I could not find at the craft store. I found that I also wanted to teach other people this wonderful process and to share my love for wax with them. But they, too, needed to be able to get the tools to create beautiful and fun pieces. So I began to create them, one at a time—there were a few fail-and-expensive attempts, but the Miriam Joy tool line began to emerge. The first one was a customized melting pot, followed by the wax tools. Then, to go along with the products, I began to provide YouTube videos for fun projects to help and inspire crafters everywhere. (See www.youtube.com/user/Miriamjoy123).

As I continue to find new ways to use the wax, I continue to make new tools. I hope to keep growing the tool line. To order Miriam Joy Products please visit me at www.MiriamJoy.com.

Note: I try to keep all the customized MJ Products made in the United States where we can also help other artists and companies grow. We have had a lot of people help us along the way, so it is important for Miriam Joy to help others.

MJ Low Temp Melting Pot

Use an MJ Low Temp Melting Pot to melt the crayons. The melting pot is UL rated and is 120°F, the perfect temperature to melt crayons without getting the wax too hot. Keeping the wax confined to the little well is what allows you to use such a small amount of crayon. The well provides an area for you to dip your wax tool. Most melting pots are round or other shapes. It would take around twenty crayons to fill up other melting pots because they do not have a well, which is what makes this process work. I have tried several other items and methods to melt my wax and have had no success when using the tools. The MJ Melting Pot is customized to keep your tool in the well.

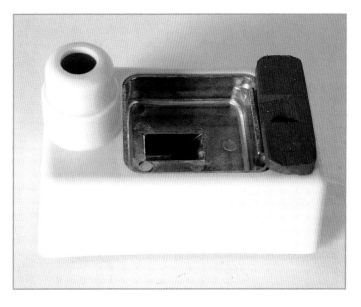

MJ Wax Design Tools

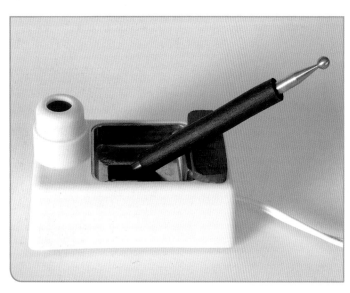

I have designed a line of MJ Wax Tools and have had them manufactured just for this process. They each have a foam handle to keep them from getting warm while being held. The foam handle also makes them comfortable to hold. The tools are well-balanced. There are four MJ Wax Design Tools. Each tool has two different sized tips, so that it is like getting two tools in each one, and who doesn't love a two for one deal?

The type of metal for these tools does matter. Aluminum tools will not work with this process, as aluminum does not hold the heat evenly and the wax does not stick to the tool. Wooden-handle tools do not hold the heat as well, and the wood handle gets very warm. After heating and cooling the wood handle tools, the tips tend to come unglued from the wood. On the MJ tool, the balls on each end hold the wax on the tool. A lot of thought and trial and error went into designing these tools. I have found that people who have had a hard time holding other tools, due to arthritis and other medical conditions, find these tools easier to use.

MJ Wax Design Tool #2 is the tool I designed first, and is still the tool I use the most and the first tool that I start my students with. If you can only start with one tool, this is the one I recommend.

- MJ Wax Design Tool #2 is $\frac{3}{16}$" on one end and $\frac{1}{4}$" on the other end. Tools bigger than this size drip a little too much.

- MJ Wax Design Tool #1 is a step down from the #2 tool. If you want a medium-sized stroke, this is a tool for you. MJ Wax Design Tool #1 is $\frac{1}{8}$" on one end and $\frac{5}{32}$" on the other end.

- MJ Wax Design Tool #0 is a smaller tool and used for smaller work. It creates smaller strokes. MJ Wax Design Tool #0 is $\frac{2}{25}$" on one end and $\frac{1}{10}$" on the other end.

- MJ Wax Design Tool #00 is the smallest of the tools. This tool is designed for fine detail work or where other strokes cannot fit. The size of the tool is $\frac{3}{64}$" on one end and .072 inches on the other end.

The size of the tool you use determines the size of the stroke or dot. If you need a larger, longer stroke or dot, use a bigger tool. If you need a little or short stroke or dot, use a smaller tool. If you need fine tiny details, use the MJ Wax Design Tool #00.

MJ Wax Design Tool sitting in melting pot

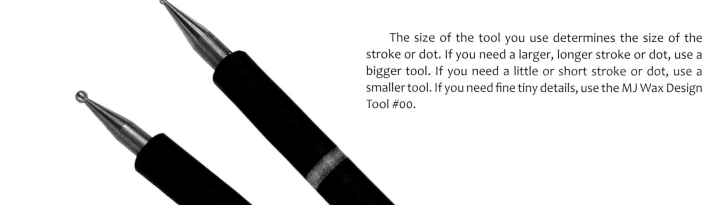

MJ Texture Brush and Insert

The MJ Texture Brush and Insert is designed to create textured backgrounds: trees, bushes, and grass. It also makes wonderful snow.

Directions: The insert is placed on top of the MJ Melting Pot when the melting pot is empty. After the insert has warmed, melt the crayon on the insert. Use your MJ Texture Brush to apply the melting crayon onto your project.

While the MJ Texture Brush was designed for wax, it works great with paints as well.

MJ Texture Brush and Insert

I have made a video to help you with this process at: **http://youtu.be/1oORrPRGOBo**

Sit the insert into the empty melting pot.

Allow the insert to warm.

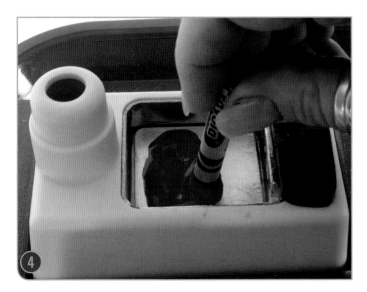

Apply a layer of crayon across the insert.

Pounce the MJ Texture Brush into the melted crayon.

11

MJ Wax Brushes

MJ Wax Brushes were designed to apply a layer of melted wax.

Directions: The brush is dipped into the well of the melting pot to pick up wax. This is one of the times that you can fill the melting pot above the well if you like. While the wax is still warm, apply it to your project. You can apply a second coat if needed. Let the first coat harden or cool and then reapply.

You do use more wax with this method. I do not clean these brushes. They are inexpensive enough to keep one for each color. I have also added foam to this brush to make it easier to handle and to keep it from getting warm. To straighten the bristles when using a brush with cold wax in the bristles, set the brush into the well of the melting pot to re-warm the wax.

There is a video to help you with this process at:
http://youtu.be/mp7rpBmRAS0

Load your MJ Wax Brush with wax from the melting pot well.

Glass Eyedroppers

There are times when the brushes and MJ Wax Tools are just not enough. The glass eyedropper applies the wax more thickly and can reach places you cannot. They are great for making thicker lines. This is one of the times that you can fill the melting pot above the well if you like.

Directions: Set the glass eyedropper into the well with the melting crayon and let it warm. It is important that you use a *glass* eyedropper. Plastic ones will melt. Push in the rubber bulb to bring the melted crayon into the tube. Then apply wax onto your project.

This is another item that is inexpensive enough that you can keep one for each color. You *can* clean them out, but it takes time. Make sure when you are done with the glass eyedropper that you squeeze the bulb and get all of the wax out. You do not want the wax to dry up in the bulb. This causes the bulb to harden; then you cannot squeeze melted wax up or out the glass tube.

There is a video to help you with this process at:
http://youtu.be/cv5MiEg4-wc

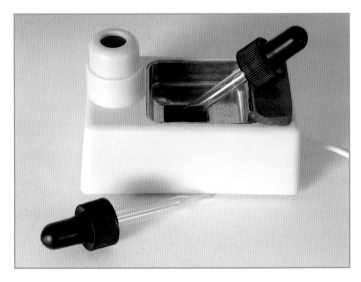

MJ Three Pot Tray

I've designed a tray that holds the melting pots in place. This makes the melting pots more secure and less likely to move. I suggest you place the electrical cords going away from you so that you do not get tangled up in them. Then hook them up to a single power cord with multiple outlets and an on/off switch on the cord so you can turn them on and off with ease at the same time. The red light on the power strip also lets you know if the melting pots are still on.

The tray has a lip to help keep everything contained. The tray helps keep the wax off you. If the wax is going to drip, it will most likely drip here. By the way, I recommend working in an old shirt or an apron since crayon is hard to get out of your clothes.

There is a video to help you with this process at:
http://youtu.be/6oIoXDV-Iq8

MJ Dry Board

The MJ Dry Board has little plastic spikes so that you can continue to dry your project after you have colored or varnished it without the project sticking to the board.

Directions: You should not spray varnish on the MJ Dry Board. Varnish the project first and then place it onto the board to continue drying.

There is a video to help you with this process at:
http://youtu.be/Mu9uv_dtJoA

Load wax into an MJ Wax Liner.

MJ Wax Liner

The wax liner is used for those times when you really need to make a straight line. You can write with it, make very small dots, or use it to outline your artwork to make it look fresh. It makes great pine needles for trees.

Directions: Place the wax liner into the melting pot well with melted wax; allow it to warm for forty-five seconds to a minute. Once warm, scoop up the wax and tool and you are ready to begin your project. As long as you warmed your tool long enough,

you will be able to write for quite a while before it stops. When the wax runs out, or the wax cools, set the wax liner back into the well to re-warm. To clean the tool, dump all of the wax out. Wipe the outside with a paper towel. Take a Q-tip and push it into the well of the wax liner to remove any remaining wax.

There is a video to help you with this process at:
http://youtu.be/5GcYQNMhdAo

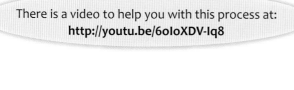

MJ Craft Templates

MJ Craft Templates were invented first, out of my frustration at not being able to create the perfect shape; and second, out of my desire to find a better way to create designs or trace more exacting patterns. While other templates are made of plastic or paper and are contained all on one sheet, the MJ Craft Templates are made of flexible rubber and can be used on round or square objects. They are the first templates that can go around the corner of a wall. These templates are great for many crafting needs, such as school projects, quilting, woodworking, stained-glass work and gourding—just to name a few. The MJ Craft Templates are made of $\frac{1}{16}$"-rubber and come in a variety of shapes and sizes. The rubber allows the templates to hold in place without slipping while tracing the shape.

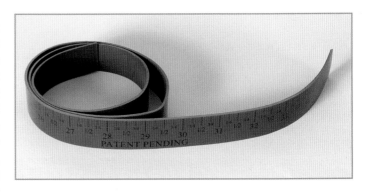

There is a video to show you how to use the craft templates at:
http://youtu.be/nc09fhVwBbY

There is also a rubber ruler, called an MJ Flex-e, that is great for measuring projects. The rubber helps hold the ruler in place so you can measure items with ease. Just place the Flex-e around the project and put a little tension on the ruler and it will hold in place while you measure.

There is a video to show you how to use the Flex-e at:
http://youtu.be/xEhY2j-zm7M

Basic Supplies

Removable Glue Dots

Removable glue dots are used when you need a little help holding the craft template in place or if the templates are larger than you can easily hold with one hand while marking. I cut the glue dots in half to fit the craft template, thus making the package of glue dots go twice as far.

Directions: Apply glue dots to at least four places on the template. Place the template on your project and trace your shape. Remove the template and pull off the glue dots. It is important to use removable glue dots: they are designed with removal in mind.

Hobby Knife with Shovel Blade

I use a hobby knife with a shovel nose blade to remove unwanted wax. It allows you to maneuver in between your strokes when removing crayon, so that if you make a mistake or if you have an unwanted drop of wax, you can simply remove it.

Directions: Always use your hobby knife at an angle when removing wax. Holding the knife with the blade straight up and down causes scratching to occur. Start at the biggest end of the stroke or drop and work toward the small end. This allows you to get under the wax more easily and you can remove more of the wax this way.

QuikWood®

QuikWood is a great two-part epoxy created to fix any wood project that needs fixing. However, I use it as a sculpting medium like clay. It has a workable time of thirty minutes and is rock-hard in an hour. The short dry time makes it great for fast, fun art projects.

Mr. Clean Magic Eraser®

I have found that a Mr. Clean Magic Eraser makes removing the charcoal pencil lines easy. They can be found in the bathroom cleaning supply section at most stores. I cut my sponge into three sections; it is a bit easier to use this way and lasts a little longer.

Directions: Wet it slightly and wring out all the water. Wipe the area that shows the charcoal pencil. This will leave a chalky white film behind. Lightly dampen a paper towel and remove the film.

There is a video to help you with this process at:
http://youtu.be/voGnUzpENYI

White Charcoal Pencil

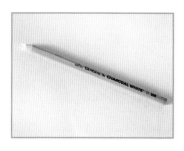

To trace the shapes onto a project, I use a white charcoal pencil. It leaves a bright enough line to see easily and can be removed. Unlike some craft pencils, you can put the charcoal pencil in a pencil sharpener to sharpen it.

Directions: If the pencil is not leaving a dark enough line, simply take the pencil and use a flame from a cigarette lighter, or other type of flame, to warm the pencil tip. This makes that pencil line bright and removes any wax buildup that you may have on the pencil.

Embossing Tool

The embossing tool is also called a heat gun, and can be found in the scrapbook section of the craft stores. Use the embossing tool to reheat the wax in a method I call twice melted, or for heat setting any base coat that uses inks or dyes.

Cleanup Supplies

Of course, the most important items are the cleanup supplies. These make cleaning a breeze. Cotton balls are used to absorb the crayon and clean the MJ Melting Pot. Cotton swabs are used to clean the MJ Wax Liner. Damp Q-tips can also be used to remove charcoal pencil lines in hard-to-get-to areas. Paper towels are used to wipe and clean your MJ Wax Design Tools as well as to clean the MJ Texture Brush and Insert.

Acrylic Paints

I work with acrylic paints the most and base-coat a lot of my projects with them. I love to work with acrylic paints; they are easy to use, dry fast, and are water-based for an easy cleanup.

Directions: You may need to base-coat a few layers of paint to get the paint even. You can also add a little water to your paint and apply a wash. This makes a nice thinner layer of paint.

Alcohol Inks

Alcohol inks are another of my favorites to work with. They come in a variety of colors; you can find them in the scrapbooking section of your craft store. They are easy to use and blend well with each other.

Varnish, Glaze, Lacquer, and Epoxy Resin

For the wax process, I use different finishes for different projects, depending on how much the project is going to be handled, or if the project is flat or whether it will be exposed to the sun.

Spray-on varnish works great, but a lot of people are intimidated by sprays. Do not let spray varnishes worry you—just try it. Practice until you get comfortable. Runs can be caused by getting too close or going too slowly when varnishing. Varnish in a ventilated area. If you are working outside in the sun, remember that you are working with wax and you cannot leave it in the sun to dry.

Directions: Start by shaking your can to mix the varnish. Spray about twelve inches away from your project. Start on one side of your project, working in a back-and-forth motion. Do not use a circular motion. It does not cover evenly. Place your project on the MJ Dry Board so that it can continue to dry without sticking to the project. Once the varnish dries to the touch, apply another coat. Applying varnish not only protects the wax, but also brings out the color of the wax (crayon). Apply at least two to three coats.

The humidity can cause your varnish to turn white. That is why I like to use gloss. It is less likely to turn white. If your varnish should turn white, let it dry and varnish it again on a dryer day to turn it back to its original state.

You can use brush-on varnish if you have used acrylic paint or have heat set your dyes so they will not run. Brush-on varnish can pick up the dye or color and bring it over your wax, so make sure that, when using it, your color has been heat set before you apply your wax design. Brush-on varnishes are usually thicker and result in better coverage.

I use glazes and lacquer on glass projects. It seems to go on well and does not show too much. I also use it over jewelry pieces to keep them from melting in the sun. The surface needs to be flat, and a thick layer of the glaze or lacquer needs to be applied. All of the wax must be covered. This sometimes can take more than one coat. Apply it by starting on the outside and working your way toward the middle. You can also apply it by putting it into a bowl and brushing it on.

Epoxy resin is heat- and waterproof. You need to be able to apply it to a flat project. This will protect the wax and keep it from melting. The epoxy resin consists of two parts and you need to follow the manufacturer's instructions. It will give you a very thick and glossy finish. Do not apply epoxy resin over twice-melted wax where the project is solid wax. The resin does not have anything to adhere to and it will peel off the wax.

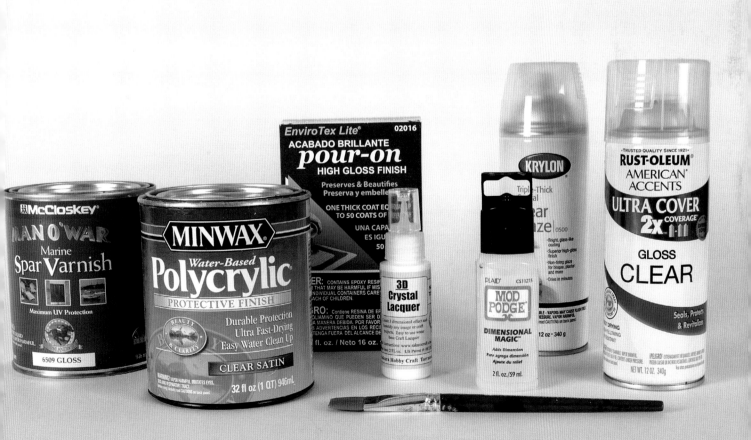

Chapter 2

Learning the Basics of Wax Design

Setting Up Your Tray

1.
Place your MJ Low Temp Melting Pots into the tray.

Place the cords away from you to keep yourself from getting tangled in them. I use a power strip to keep the melting pots plugged into, so that I do not have to unplug all of the melting pots individually. I can just flip the switch and turn them off and on. If you have a red light on the power strip, it helps to keep track whether they are off or on.

Fold your paper towel into fours. Place it in the right-hand bottom corner and place your tools on top.

To the left of the bottom tray, keep the craft knife and white charcoal pencil so they will always be handy.

18

2.

Next, plug in your MJ Low Temp Melting Pot and get it warmed up. This only takes a few minutes, and you can load your crayon while it is still warming. Remember to use only Crayola brand crayons. (I will refer to Crayola crayons as wax, which is what they are.)

Holding the crayon with the tip pointed up, cut the crayon paper just above the word "Crayola."

3.

With your hobby knife, cut the paper down the side of the crayon to where you first cut the paper. Do not try to peel the paper back with the knife. It is much harder that way and you are more likely to cut yourself.

4.

Peel the paper off the crayon to where you cut it with the hobby knife. I leave the rest of the paper on my crayon. This keeps it clean and keeps from getting other colors on the crayon. I also leave the name of the crayon as the last part so that if I need to know what color it is, I have that information.

5.

Take your scissors and cut the crayon just above where you cut the paper.

6.

Cut that piece in half with your scissors. By breaking the crayon into two pieces, they fit into the well of the melting pot. It keeps the crayon from melting on the top layer of the well and wasting your wax.

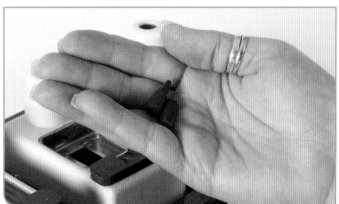

7.

Put both pieces into the well. It is okay to get some of the crayon on the next level of the well—it just helps to keep it cleaner and avoids waste.

There is a video you can watch to show you how to cut and add the crayon at:
http://youtu.be/64wt_GAWB3s

Your melted crayon should not overflow into the second level.

8.

Your melted crayon should not overflow into the second level. You want to make sure that you do not fill the well too full unless you are working with the glass eyedropper or the MJ Wax Brushes. If the well is so full that you cannot see the rectangle of the well, you will start to drip more when working with the MJ Wax Tools. If you fill the well too full, simply take a cotton ball and absorb a little crayon.

There is a video to help you know if you have too much crayon in the well at:
http://youtu.be/S6bcOZJoIZg

9.

It is important to keep the well full. Do not let your well get less than three-quarters full. This helps keep your strokes the same size because you are picking up the same amount of wax. If you notice your strokes getting smaller, check the level of your wax.

10.

To add crayon to your well, take your scissors and cut the size of crayon piece you may need. I leave the paper on when I am doing this. A lot of times once it is cut, it comes out of the paper all by itself; if not, then cut the paper with your hobby knife and remove it.

There is a video to help you know when to add more crayon to your well at:
http://youtu.be/LBQatFU1dnY

Absorb just a little crayon with the cotton ball if the well is too full.

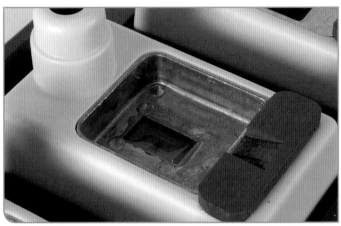

The right amount of wax in the well.

The level of wax when you need to add more crayon.

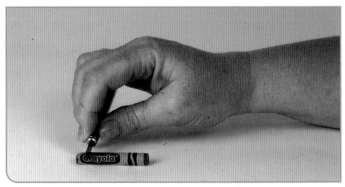

Keep the well full by adding more crayon as needed.

Loading Your Tool

1.

THIS IS THE MOST IMPORTANT INFORMATION TO MAKE THIS PROCESS WORK! If you do not warm your tools and try to apply warm wax with a cold tool, you will get a glob of wax. The wax will stick to the tool and not want to come off. It only takes about fifteen seconds or more to warm the tool. If the area you are working in is cooler, the tool may need a few seconds longer to warm.

2.

Make sure that the project you are working on is not cold. This will cause the wax not to work correctly. If your item is cold, allow it to warm up to room temperature. You can also warm it up with a blow dryer or embossing tool.

Start with the small end of the MJ Wax Design Tool #2. This is the easier of the tools to begin with.

3.

Place the tool into your wax and warm the end of your tool.

4.

Once your MJ Wax Design Tool is warm, place it in the deepest part of the well. Go all the way to the bottom. Touch the bottom and pull your tool straight out. By pulling it straight up, you get the maximum amount of wax. Do not pull the tool out slowly or come up along the side of the well. This removes some of the wax.

Watch yourself the first few times you load your strokes, as it is an instinct to want to knock off the drip of wax. You want the drip. The drip is what adds texture to your stroke. You will not even know that you are doing this. Be careful not to form bad habits of stirring the drip, clicking the sides, or hitting it. The crayon should only be stirred if it has been sitting a while and the color has separated in the wax. White crayons need stirring a little more often, as do metallic and glitter crayons. The easiest way to do this is to not over-think it. Just go to the deepest part of the well, touch the bottom, and pull the tool straight out. Make sure that you load it in the same spot each time, as this will keep your strokes consistent in size.

5.

Know where you are going with your stroke before you pick it up. Do not load the wax and sit there and hold it while you are looking where to go. This cools your wax and your stroke will not go on smoothly. It is natural to get excited after putting on a stroke—while still holding the tool in your hand and allowing the tool to cool. Watch out for this. (I am the worst offender of holding the tool in my hand while talking to someone.) If you get distracted, just let the tool warm up again before your next stroke.

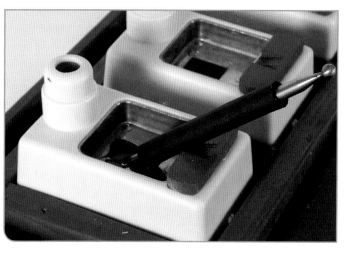

Warm your tools by placing them in the wax.

Place your tool in the deepest part of the well and pull straight up.

6.

Keep the project you are working on no farther than twelve inches from the melting pot. Any farther and your tool will start to cool off. If you notice a drip, see how far your project is from the melting pot. If drips continue, check to see if you are sitting in front of a breeze, like that from a fan, heater, or air conditioner.

There is a video to help you with this process at:
http://youtu.be/7TWjiINf3kQ

How to Make a Stroke

1.

Pick up a pencil and hold it in your hand as if you are going to write on something. See how you are holding the pencil sideways, while resting your hand on the paper. This is how you should hold the tool. By resting the side of your hand on your project surface, you gain control of the stroke. Do not try to hold your tool straight up and down or try to balance it with your little finger. Resting the heel of your hand will give you balance, you will have control over your stroke, and your lines will come out consistently straight. If you try to make the strokes with the tool straight up and down, without resting your hand on the surface, your strokes will wobble all over the place. Now pull the pencil toward you in a straight line.

2.

Start by practicing your strokes on a piece of paper. Load your tool with the wax: going to the deepest part of the well, touch the bottom and bring it straight out. Bring it to your paper. Make sure that you do not go too fast. This will cause the wax to drip. With your hand sideways, like you would hold a pencil, and your hand resting on the paper, pull the stroke toward you. Like brush work, you should pull your strokes directly toward you. Slowly set the tool on the paper, pulling it toward you until it runs out of wax. Most people lift the tool too early. Make sure you pull, pull, pull that stroke. You are starting with a bunch of wax and going until you run out of wax on the tool. Pulling the stroke until it runs out of wax results in a great tail on the stroke. Remember to always pull the stroke until it runs out or is stopped short by a pattern design.

There is a video to help you with this process at:
http://youtu.be/imRRnLwBdkw

3.

Make sure that you are pulling your stroke nice and easy. Do not skim the top of the paper with the tool. Set the tool down and pull your stroke nice and slow. Pulling it too fast makes the wax skip. The slower you pull the stroke, the longer the stroke will become. If you notice that the edges of your strokes are uneven and are not smooth, you need to warm your tool a little more. Make sure when you are pulling your stroke that you do not twist the tool. This picks up wax from the back and makes the tail of the stroke uneven. Never go back over a stroke you do not like. The wax is already cooling and it will just make a mess.

There is a video to help you with this process at:
http://youtu.be/PH8tSEQYBJo

4.

Remember that the length and the width of the stroke are controlled by the size of the tool you use: the bigger the tool, the bigger the stroke; the smaller the tool, the smaller the stroke. You must reload for each stroke no matter how big or small the stroke is.

How to Make a Dot

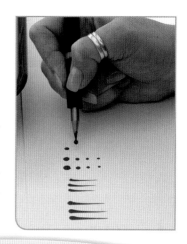

Dots are loaded the same as a stroke. The size of the tool determines the size of the dot. Load the tool each time you make a dot. Do not think that you can load your tool anywhere in the well. Make sure that you go to the bottom of the well when loading the wax. This helps keep the dots consistent in size. You can also do a descending dot, which is a lot of fun. Load your tool and dot, dot, dot. Each successive dot will be smaller because you are running out of wax. I use this method a lot in my designs. You can do designs with just dots. You will also notice little tiny flecks of wax when you do the dots. The bigger the dot, the more flecks you get. If you are getting more than two flecks per dot, then slow down. You can remove them with your hobby knife or leave them depending on the texture of your design. Apply dots to areas that need cleaning up, like the ends of strokes or to help fill in an open area.

There is a video to help you with this process at:
http://youtu.be/7fGqF5YDpMI

Removing a Stroke, Dot, or Drop

Use a shovel tip on the hobby knife to remove a stroke, dot, or drop. The shovel tip lets you get in between your strokes and remove the wax you do not want. Allow the wax to harden or cool. Trying to remove wax while it is liquid is harder and can smear the color of the crayon, making a bigger mess to clean up.

1.
Put the hobby knife under the largest part of the stroke or dot. Starting with the largest part of the stroke will get a bigger piece of the wax off.

Always hold the hobby knife at an angle. Do not hold the knife straight up and down or scratches will occur. Turn the knife to the other angle to remove the tail part of the stroke.

2.
When you are removing the wax, you should not be able to hear any sound. If you hear scraping sounds, try a lighter touch.

If you need to remove any stain left behind from the wax, do so with a gum eraser. If you are going to put a stroke back on, do not worry about the stain, unless it would show.

There is a video to help you with this process at:
http://youtu.be/fGNg21bfb2A

Practice Makes Perfect

You should practice until you are comfortable with your strokes, dots, and drops. Also practice removing them. Try different tools to make different sized strokes and dots. Some people find that a certain size tool works better for them and is easier to use. Make sure that you try both ends of each MJ Wax Design Tool.

Know that each Crayola color will work differently. The darker colors contain more pigments and will make bigger strokes because they are thicker. The thinner colors, like yellow, will be thin, but you can pull the stroke farther. Learn the colors and how they work. Thinner colors can also drip a little more. Take the colors that you want to use and pull them with each tool so that you know how long that color will pull and what size stroke it will make.

Practice until your strokes become consistent in size. The more you practice, the better your strokes will become. Remember to load the tool in the well in the same way every time. If your strokes start to get smaller, check the crayon level in the well.

Remember that you are your own worst critic. If you do not like a stroke, then remove it. If it bugs you, take it off.

There is a good video that helps you with all the basics and is a good refresher course at:
http://youtu.be/cR5Tmi-kJ5E

Chapter 3

Cleaning Your Tools

How to Clean the MJ Wax Design Tools

Cleaning your MJ Wax Design Tools is easy. Simply take a paper towel and wipe off the tool while it is still warm. You will need to do this before you use a new color. It you let the wax harden on the tool, removing the wax becomes difficult. Place your tool back into the wax to warm it again and wipe it on the paper towel. I keep my paper towel folded into fours, making it easier to use.

How to Clean the MJ Melting Pot

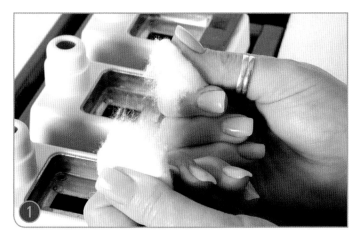

1.

To change colors or clean your melting pot, simply take a cotton ball and pull it in half. Keep it in balls.

2.

Take the first half of the cotton ball and place it into the well. I use the MJ Wax Design Tool #0, because it can get into tight corners. Do not touch the metal with your fingers. The metal is hot. Using the wax tool, slowly push the cotton ball into the well. If you push the cotton ball too fast, the color comes out the sides, making a bigger mess. Going slower allows the wax to absorb as it goes. Lift the cotton ball out with your wax tool. Start at the front of the well, get under the cotton ball, and pull it out.

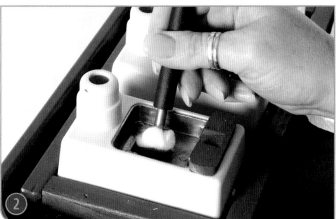

3.

Take the other half of the cotton ball and, using the wax tool, clean off the top part of the well. Finish by cleaning the inside of the well. You will be amazed how easy it is to clean. The cleaning is done while the melting pot is still plugged in.

Once you have cleaned the well, you can put your new color into the well to melt.

4.

The crayon can be left in the well and used again later. Just plug the melting pot back in when you are ready to use it and wait for it to melt before you start. If you are done with the color, unplug the melting pot and let the color cool. When the wax is hard, plug the melting pot back in. It will start to melt on the sides. This happens very fast. Take your hobby knife and push it between the top of the well and the color will pop out in a block.

You can reuse the color block. It never goes bad. Just pop it in a bag and use it next time. To reuse it, start by adding the block of color to your melting pot first then add any additional wax needed to fill the well.

There is a video to help you with this process at:
http://youtu.be/FKQKi-Y9lhs

How to Clean the MJ Texture Brush

1.

To clean your MJ Texture Brush, start by melting the crayon in your brush on the insert.

2.

To clean the MJ Texture Brush and Insert, wipe the insert while in the melting pot with a paper towel.

3.

Set the MJ Texture Brush on the insert to melt the crayon. Wipe the MJ Texture Brush on the paper towel. Keep repeating until the crayon is melted out.

4.

To clean the brush completely, spray with a degreaser like Awesome®. Clean the brush again on the insert in the melting pot until all the color is gone. Rinse with warm water.

There is a video to help you with this process at:
http://youtu.be/qwwYk4_agoE

26

Chapter 4

Basic Wax Designs

Basic Shapes

Circles

Out of all my artwork, I use circle designs the most. There is something about them. So let's start with a circle.

Tips

- Remember not to go over a stroke if you do not like it or the size. Remove it and start again.

- Another rule is not to cross over the top half of a stroke. The wax is thicker there and you are running into cold wax. You can cross over the bottom half of the stroke where the wax is thinner.

1.

Using the MJ Craft Templates, large circles, pull out the two smallest of these. Lay them down on your paper one inside of the other. Hold them in place with your hand. Trace the inside circle with a pencil.

2.

Remove the smallest remaining template, while still holding the second template in place. Now trace around the inside of the second template.

3.

With your pencil, place a dot in the center of the circle. You are going to pull your stroke from the circle to the dot.

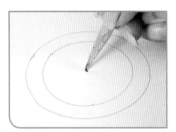

4.

Use the small end of an MJ Wax Design Tool #1. Starting on the inside circle, pull the stroke toward you until you reach the center dot or run out of wax.

5.

Turn your paper around, so the stroke is now on the bottom, and pull the next stroke from the top, again to the center dot.

6.

You have divided the circle into half; now divide it into quarters. Move your paper around a half turn and pull the stroke toward you to the center dot.

7.

Repeat on the other side.

8.

I always do circles by dividing them. It keeps the strokes more even. Now that you have done four strokes, divide the circle into eight strokes. Start by going in between the strokes that you just did, right in the middle.

9.

Complete your circle by always going to the right. This helps you to keep your place and not lose a stroke. You should now have a circle with eight strokes. Turn your paper with each stroke so you are always pulling from the top to the middle.

10.

If you had a smaller circle, you could stop with eight strokes. But to really fill the space and give it a great design, put a total of sixteen strokes in this design. Start again, in between the last strokes.

11.

Continue your strokes around the circle, remembering to go to your right. Turn the paper so that you are pulling each stroke toward you. With a little practice, you will have a nice circle. Make sure that you are

setting your hand completely down and resting it on the paper to give you the most control over the stroke. Now try bigger circles and smaller circles. Change the tool for the size stroke you need. Try different color crayons, see how they pull differently?

There is a video to help you with this process at:
http://youtu.be/zxw6f8pZwbg

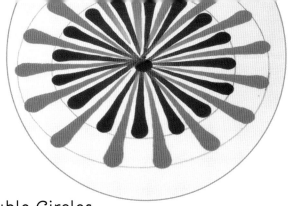

Double Circles

Take your circle to the next level by turning it into a double circle. This will teach you how to build on a basic design. Switch to the MJ Wax Design Tool #2 small end. This helps fill up the pattern. Most people do not think that the stroke will fit between the smaller strokes. The fattest part of the stroke is above the smaller circle.

12.

Start at the second circle and pull the stroke down between each stroke. Pull the stroke until it runs out of wax or you reach the center. Do not worry if you run into the wax on the smaller circle.

13.

Complete your strokes by going to the right, moving your paper so that you pull the stroke from the top toward you. You should have a total of sixteen strokes in this second row.

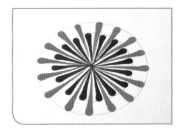

14.

To clean up the tails of the strokes in the center, add a dot to the center. You can pull strokes out from the circle; you can add dots or descending dots. How do you see the design? What can you change or add? If you do a very small circle in the center, you may want to work with the circle on the outside first. Then complete the smaller circle. This would keep the smaller circle cleaner.

You can use this method and apply it to any shape including squares, diamonds, and ovals. It makes the design less overwhelming if you break it down. It also helps keep the pattern more even.

Square

1

Start by drawing a square with the MJ Craft Templates. Trace the design on the inside of the square.

2.

With a pencil, place a dot at the center so you know where your strokes should end.

3.

Unlike the circle, a square gives you a great starting place. Start in the corner of the square. Pull the stroke from the top corner to the center dot or until you run out of wax. As you can see, I ran out of wax before reaching the dot. This is okay; just pull the stroke as long as you can toward the center.

4.

Now turn the square so the next corner is on top. Pull the stroke from the top corner to the center of the square.

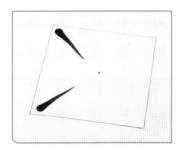

5.

Turn the square again and repeat this step.

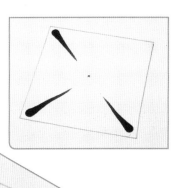

6.

Pull your stroke in the last corner of the square, giving you a total of four strokes.

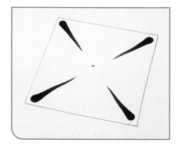

7.

You are going to divide the square again: pull a stroke in between each of the corners. This stroke will be closer to the center dot. Remember to move your paper so the stroke is on top each time.

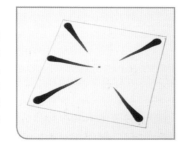

8.

Complete the square for a total of eight strokes. Turn the paper to your right as you are working to help you keep your place.

9.

There is still quite a bit of room in between the strokes. There's not enough room to divide it off evenly two more times for a total of three strokes in between each of the current strokes, but there is enough room to add two strokes in between.

10.

Add two strokes in between each of the strokes in your square. Work toward the right so you do not lose your place until you have completed the square.

This should get you thinking about how to add strokes to a design. You can add one or two strokes in between other strokes depending on the space you need to fill. Try a bigger square; try a smaller square. Once you master that, try a double square. How about adding dots to it, or pulling strokes out away from the square?

There is a video to help you with this process at:
http://youtu.be/lal16Rrch8A

Freehand Designs

Fleur-de-Lis

Once you have gotten shapes down, let's work on a little more freehand strokes. You cannot pull a stroke across the top of a stroke because the wax is cold and hard. You can, however, pull a stroke into a stroke and combine their tails. Start with the simple fleur-de-lis.

1.

Pull a stroke down the center. If you need to draw your lines on to follow, do so with the white charcoal pencil or regular pencil. These lines will be covered with your stroke, so you will not need to remove them.

2.

If you want a larger design, use a larger tool; if you want a smaller design, use a smaller tool. I am using an MJ Wax Design Tool #2. Pull a stroke from the right and meet up with the first stroke about halfway down, then pull the stroke into the end of the tail. Repeat on the left side.

3.

Easy right? Now you are going to add on to that. Pull a stroke along the bottom right of the design, the tail meeting up with the design in the center. Repeat that stroke on the left side.

4.

Add another set of strokes above the bottom ones. Start the set just a little closer to the center than the one you just did. Pull it until you meet up at the center end. Repeat the stroke on the left side.

5.

Dots add so much to a design. Finish this design off by adding descending dots to the top of the first stroke. Then clean up the design by adding a dot to the bottom where the tails meet.

There is a video to help you with this process at:
http://youtu.be/sP9xooAWlOk

Rolling Wave

1.

If you need to draw the basic design with a pencil and follow it with your tool, that is okay. Start a stroke by setting it down and curving it to the right, then left and pull the tail out, coming

back toward the middle. If you do this stroke in the other direction it creates an "S." You may find one direction easier to do than the other direction. Each stroke should start in the curved part of the tail in the stroke above it. The more you practice, the easier it will become.

2.

To complete this design, add dots to it. You can add the dots on the top right of the design, or add them to the left of the design, or both.

Crashing Wave

1.

Start your stroke by pulling it curved over and down. The next stroke will start near the top of the prior stroke; curve it over and down just like the last one. Continue adding strokes until you have completed the area you need to fill.

2.

As always, you can add dots. I have placed my dots inside the design. You can place them above the design or in both places.

These basics can add so much to a project. Start with the basic designs and build on them. Put some of them together.

There is a video to help you with this process at:
http://youtu.be/Y9liiwqB9Fs

There is a video to help you with this process at:
http://youtu.be/Fh-DdR_QBk4

Leaves

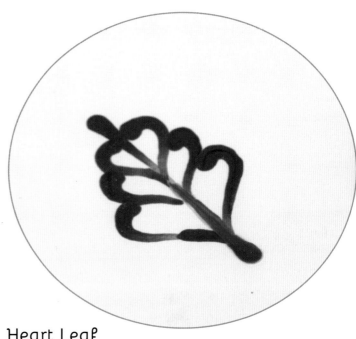

Basic Leaf

You are going to learn some different leaves that you can use by themselves or with flowers (changing the whole look of the flower). Different colors in a leaf can change the color of it as well.

1.

Starting with green wax, using the MJ Wax Design Tool #2 small end, pull a stroke out from the right side curving around and pulling it until it runs out of wax. Pull a stroke out from the left side curving it until it runs out of wax, meeting up with the first stroke.

2.

Change the color to yellow green. Switch to the MJ Wax Design Tool #1, pull the stroke starting at the top of the leaf, and pull until you run out of wax near the tip of the leaf. You can create a leaf just like this.

3.

Switching to the MJ Wax Design Tool #0—you can use either end, depending on the size you may want the veins—start at the top of the center stroke and set your tool down. Pull your tool up and out. This helps give you a smaller stroke with a point. You are not pulling the stroke the whole way out unless you have room. Continue adding small strokes down the center stroke and repeat on the other side.

Heart Leaf

Let's move on to a fancier leaf. This is my favorite leaf. It can add a lot to a simple flower. Keep this leaf in mind if you have a bigger space that you need to fill in.

1.

You are going to start at the opposite direction for this leaf. Pull your first stroke in, beginning where the leaf will end. Make sure you allow enough room for the leaf. Pull the stroke until you run out of wax. The size of the wax tool you use depends on the size you want the leaf to be.

2.

Starting on the left side, start the stroke a little from the top and pull the stroke out toward the left, curving down, and pull until you meet the tail of the first stroke.

3.

Now go to the right side and repeat. The two strokes that you just made should look like a heart.

There is a video to help you with this process at:
http://youtu.be/esPy-e3eFgo

4.

Pull the next row of strokes the same way, except you will pull these out a little farther than you did the last ones. This makes your leaf fatter.

5.

Continue with the rows on the leaf until you fill in the space or you are running out of wax before you get to the center stroke.

There is a video to help you with this process at:
http://youtu.be/qKzUlCvetxY

Fern Leaf

The third leaf you're about to learn is a fern leaf. It's a group of small leaves, all connected.

1.

Draw a line down the center of your fern leaf, so you know where to attach each leaflet. This is a slightly different stroke. You have been using it in the veins of your earlier leaves. Set your tool down and pull it up, making a point at the tip. Do not pull the stroke out long. Reload each time.

2.

Start next to your line at the bottom and work your way up on the left side.

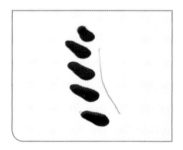

3.

Come back and complete the strokes on the right side of the line. Remember that nature is not perfect. Leaves are not all the same size. Once you get comfortable with the strokes, you may want to use a bigger tool for the bottom leaflets and go smaller as you work your way up.

4.

You can create very small leaflets at the top using the MJ Wax Design Tool #0 or #00 tool, or you can use the wax liner to create more of a whimsical feel. Make sure that you have warmed your wax tool long enough. Start at the bottom and bring it into a curl at the top.

There is a video to help you with this process at:
http://youtu.be/qj-oNgjGBT4

Flowers

Little Rose

1.

To make the rose a little easier, start with a basic drawing. Draw a dot in the middle and a line coming in from the left side curving around the dot. Draw a line coming in from the right side followed by another one coming in from the left.

2.

Since this is a small rose, use a smaller tool. If you want it bigger, use a larger tool. Start by pulling the first stroke in from the left. Stop the tail at the end of the line you have drawn.

3.

Just underneath the tail of the last stroke, pull a stroke in from the right.

4.

Go back to the left side and pull another stroke in from the left to complete the rose. Keep the strokes close together to make the rose look like a rose. Add a dot to the center top of the rose.

5.

Changing to a green color for the stem, pull a stroke using a larger tool from the center bottom of the rose downward. Pull it nice and slow so that you get a nice long stem.

6.

Pull a stroke from each side of the center stem. These strokes can be a little smaller. They are the leaves for the rose. See how sweet and simple that was?

There is a video to help you with this process at:
http://youtu.be/RoBTeP61vi8

Large Rose

1.

Start with a dot in the center of the rose. Using a smaller tool, pull three strokes close around the dot. Flower petals are usually in odd numbers so to make your flowers more pleasing to the eye, try to create flowers with five and seven petals.

You can draw your pattern first if you need to boost your confidence and to assist with placement. Just for an example of size, I used a larger tool for the center dot and used an MJ Wax Design Tool #0, large end for the first row.

2.

I used an MJ Wax Design Tool #1 large end for this row. Learn to adjust for the size of rose you want. Put five strokes around the rose. Keep the strokes close to the first row of petals.

3.

Move up to a larger size tool and create the next row of petals with six or seven strokes. Keep the strokes close to the previous row of petals. I used an MJ Wax Design Tool #2, small end, for this row. I did not worry about which direction I pulled my rose petals. You can, however, pull them going a different direction, starting at the middle of the rose. This makes it look like it is blooming from the center. Play with that. Find what you like. Do not be afraid to find your own style.

4.

Now pull a green curved stroke out from the side of the rose. Pull the stroke until it runs out of wax. I used an MJ Wax Design Tool #2, small end, for the leaf.

5.

Pull a petal from the other side of the leaf. Pull it until you run out of wax while joining it up with the tail of the other stroke. Move your paper or project so that you are pulling the petal toward you. It is easier to pull a stroke toward you.

6.

Now pull a stroke down the middle to complete your leaf.

This is the basic leaf. Use leaves to fill in where you might have a hole or gap in the rose.

There is a video to help you with this process at:
http://youtu.be/NnbzchQUaxs.

Rose Bud

How about a rose bud? If you need to start with a drawing outline, do so. In these photos, I am starting with a smaller tool: I'm using the MJ Wax Design Tool #0 large end. This is an example only; practice with different tools, for whatever size rose bud you need.

1.

Pull the stroke on the top back petal. You can pull the stroke either direction.

2.

Pull the next petal going the opposite direction, meeting up at the tail of the first stroke, forming a small oval or circle.

3.

You can stick with the same tool or if you feel that you need to move up to a large tip, do so. I used the MJ Wax Design Tool #1 small end for the sides of the bud. Pull a stroke out from the bottom of the rose bud curving up the right side until you meet the top right side. Repeat on the left side.

4.

Switch to your leaf color. With the same tool (unless you feel like using a different one!), pull a stroke up from the bottom center of the rose bud up to the top.

5.

Pull a leaf from the bottom center of the rose bud out to the right side. Pull until you run out of wax. Repeat on the left side.

6.

Switch to a larger tool, which allows you to pull the stroke longer. I am using the MJ Wax Design Tool #2 small end. Remember too that by changing to a thinner color like yellow-green, a stroke can be pulled even farther. Pull the stroke from the bottom of the rose bud down, until you run out of wax. Pull it nice and slow. Do not hurry your stroke. This will help to pull the stroke longer giving you a nice long stem. I pulled the stroke with a little curve to add to the design.

With the same tool, pull a little leaf off to the side of the stem. Do this by lifting up your tool as you start to pull it up and off your paper. You are not pulling it until it runs out of wax. This gives you a fatter, smaller leaf with more of a point.

7.

Switching to a yellow or a center color, add some dots to complete the bud. I used the MJ Wax Design Tool #1 so my biggest dot would not be too big. Go to the top circle on the bud and add some

descending dots, meaning, load your wax tool and dot, dot, dot. Each dot will be smaller than the last. This gives you different sized dots to get that pollen look in the flower.

There is a video to help you with this process at:
http://youtu.be/07FI75oifI4

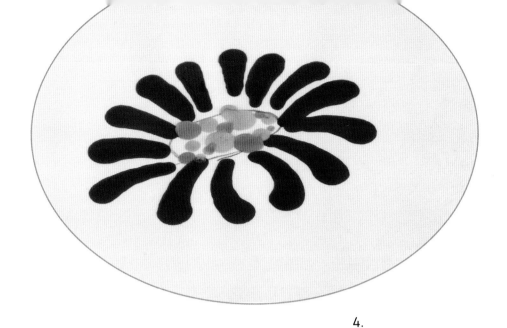

Daisy Flower

1.

Start with the center of the flower. Make it an oval shape. Use a larger tool for this flower because you want a fat petal going to a point at the end. You are going to pull the stroke just a little differently: Set the tool down and pull the wax

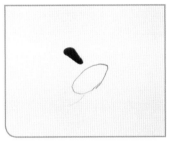

and start to lift the tool up at the end. This is similar to the stroke you did on the fern leaf, but you are pulling the stroke longer in some spots. Start the first petal at the top. Keep it close to the center.

2.

Starting at the center petal, continue to add more strokes for petals. Each one gets a little farther away from the center and has a little more curve to it.

3.

Start again at the center petal; repeat the strokes on the left side of the flower.

4.

Following the way the strokes are going, keep curving them until you reach the center bottom of the flower. Your bottom strokes can be longer or shorter.

5.

Add a first layer of dots to the center of the flower. Have the dots come into the tails of the petals just a little.

6.

Switch colors and add the second layer of dots.

Make some of your flowers have a circle center with the petals the same in size. What type of leaves do you think your flower needs? Can you add a second row of petals? Try adding long stems with the MJ Wax Liner.

There is a video to help you with this process at:
http://youtu.be/-VXs4wHdwGs

Sunflower

You are going to create a sunflower using simple strokes.

1.

Start with a center for your flower. I traced a circle using the MJ Craft Templates. The size of your tool will depend on the size of your flower. Pull a curved stroke out away from the center, until you run out of wax.

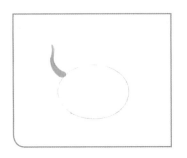

2.

Pull the other side of the petal from the center of the flower. Curving the stroke, meet up with the tail of the stroke you just made. (This is also a basic leaf pattern.)

3.

Start your second petal next to the one you just completed.

4.

Continue the petals all the way around the flower. Try to have an odd number of petals.

5.

Starting at the circle, pull strokes down the center of the petals. You could use a different color, like orange, if you want contrast.

6.

Now do a second row of petals. Start about halfway up the petals of the first row. Your bottom half of this petal is covered. Pull the stroke in between the first row and about halfway up the petals. The stroke is taller than the first row. Go to the other side and start the stroke on the other petal and pull until you meet up with the tail of the first stroke to form a petal.

7.

Continue all the way around the first row. You can add just a few petals here and there, or add a third row. Do what you think is right.

8.

Now add center veins to the second row. Start down in between the first row of petals and pull it to the top of the petals.

9.

Start adding your leaves. Use them to fill in spots that are empty. Start your leaf coming out from the first row in between the second row of petals. I like to make these leaves larger than the petals. Sunflower leaves are much bigger than the petals.

10.

Continue to add a few more leaves. Remember to add them in odd numbers. You can add them to just the top of the flower, just the bottom of the flower, or all the way around. Decide if you want a vein down the center of your petal, or whether you want smaller strokes for more veins.

11.

The center of the sunflower is made with descending dots. I use a larger tool and start by adding dots. Do not let the dots in the first layer touch until they are cool. If warm wax meets warm wax, it runs together and you lose the shape of your dots.

12.

On the second layer of dots, I used a different color. This gives the flower some depth. On a sunflower center you could use black or brown dots.

Start thinking about how you would do it differently next time. What colors would you use? By simply changing the color of a sunflower to red, you now have a poinsettia. To give it a little Christmas sparkle, add little gold wax dots to the center. What other flower could you create by changing the color? How about using the wax liner and adding a swirl to it? What would happen if you made a different colored flower and added heart leaves instead?

Have I got you thinking? It is my mission for you to take what I am teaching you and build on it. Come up with your own designs and style!

There is a video to help you with this process at:
http://youtu.be/4_ooQnux-jk

Cosmos Flower

1.

Start with a circle in the middle. You can draw your flower petals on if you need to. Start at the top center of the petal. Pull the stroke curved around and down to the flower center. Repeat on the other side of

the petal forming a heart. If your wax is still warm at the top of the petal, it will form together. That is okay for this design.

2.

Complete the petals all around until you form the flower. Leave a little room in between each petal.

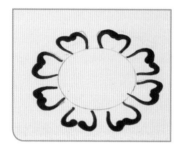

3.

Try different strokes or dots inside the flower petals. I did descending dots down the middle of the petal.

4.

I decided that there was still room in the petals to add a small stroke on each side. Would you like the petals with the strokes and not the dots?

5.

Try a dot on the top of the petal where the strokes meet.

6.

Instead of a dotted flower center this time, do a circle design. Pull your strokes one at a time from the circle to the center of the flower. Divide the strokes to form a circle. Add a dot in the center. Do you like this center better? What

other types of centers for flowers can you make? What colors would you like to try?

7.

There is still a lot of room in between the petals. Pull a stroke from about the same height as the petals, in between each of the petals to the circle center. That changes the whole look of the flower.

8.

To give it more of a whimsical feel, add some more dots. Take the descending dots out from the top middle of the flower petals. Do you like it with or without the descending dots? What would you do differently next time? What type of leaf

do you feel it needs? How can you put a flower behind this one?

Have I got you thinking yet? This is a great example of starting simple and building on it. Take what you have learned and make it your own.

There is a video to help you with this process at:
http://youtu.be/8A6moTrX4Gg

Chapter 5

Start Out Simple

Decorated Tile Magnets

1.

Start with a simple project, one that is easy to handle and flat, like a ceramic tile. Use an unsealed tile. You can use sealed tiles as well; just make sure that you use a thick varnish to keep the wax secure. For this project I used 2" tile.

2.

If the tiles are unsealed, you may need to seal them with a coat or two of spray varnish. The best way to know if you need to seal a tile is to pull a stroke on the tile. Did the stroke come out smooth? If the stroke is broken or was hard to pull, seal the tile. I used a spray varnish from Krylon® gloss to seal the tiles. It is inexpensive and dries fast. Put two coats of varnish on and try the stroke again. If it pulls smoothly, you are ready to apply the wax.

3.

Put a white dot in the center of the tile with the white charcoal pencil. With the MJ Wax Design Tool #1 large end, pull a dandelion stroke from the corner to the dot in the middle or until you run out of wax. Repeat this in each of the other three corners.

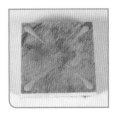

4.

Switch to the small end of the MJ Wax Design Tool #1 and pull a red stroke down and to the right of the dandelion stroke. Meet up with the tail of the dandelion stroke and pull until you reach the middle dot or run out of wax. Repeat in the remaining three corners.

5.

This design is similar to the fleur-de-lis. Pull a stroke from the left side of the dandelion stroke to the middle dot. Repeat in each of the other three corners.

6.

With the MJ Wax Design Tool #0 large end, pull a black stroke in between the red strokes. Repeat on the other three sides of the tile.

7.

Pull a stroke down and to the right of the black stroke you just did. Meet up with the tail of the first stroke and pull to the middle dot. Repeat on the other three sides of the tile.

8.

Pull a stroke down and to the left of the middle stroke. Repeat on the other three sides of the tile.

9.

I added a stone in the center of the tile. You could put a dot of wax in the middle if you are not going to add a stone. (Don't glue a stone on top of a dot of wax; the stone will come off.)

See how easy it was to do a basic design? Try some other basic designs on tiles. How about a rose? Leaves work great to fill in an open area. Three descending dots make great fillers too.

Make a set of six magnets for your refrigerator, or as a gift.

To make a magnet out of the design....

1.

...take one of the prominent colors used on the design and find a matching acrylic paint. Paint the sides of the magnet. I sealed my tiles with epoxy resin. Place the tile on something that elevates it and the resin can run off the sides. I used a "Popsicle" stick to spread it around and make sure all the areas were covered. Wipe any resin off the bottom of the tile. Make sure that all the wax—especially dots because they stick out higher—is completely covered with the epoxy resin. Allow to dry. By covering it with resin, it is waterproof, heat-proof, and hopefully drop-proof.

2.

Allow the resin to dry. Glue on a heavy-duty magnet with E6000®. Make sure you glue the right side of the magnet to the tile. E6000 is a great glue for hard-to-glue items, like rock, glass, plastic, and so on. Allow the glue to completely set for twenty-four hours.

Rock Butterfly

I love to use rocks as the home for a favorite design, a butterfly, or a dragonfly. We all have rocks or can find rocks. Look outside, at the lake or the beach. Find a smooth, flat rock that will fit the design you have in mind.

These make great paperweights: office gifts that people can set on their desks. What does the person like? What is his or her favorite color? Turn a rock into a special present just for them.

Start by varnishing your rock with a couple of coats of spray varnish. You should be able to pull a smooth stroke on its surface.

1.

If needed, draw your design on the rock with a white charcoal pencil.

2.

To do the butterfly body, I use the MJ Wax Design Tool #2 large end. (Be careful not to drip—because you are picking up more wax, it can drip a little more.) Pull the stroke slow, making it nice and long. I did the body with black; use any color you want.

You'll notice that a rock pulls differently than paper or a tile. It may be a little rougher. Each item you work with will be a little different.

3.

Using the same tool, add a dot on top of the large body stroke. This is the head of the butterfly.

4.

Use the MJ Wax Design Tool #0 to pull the small strokes for the antennae. Put a little curve in them. Pull them out, meeting up with the head of the butterfly.

5.

I decided that I would use robin's egg crayon for the color of the butterfly...but what color do you like? What color would stand out well on the color of the rock you are using?

    Starting with the wing behind, pull a curved stroke from the top of that wing, to the body. Use a wax tool that will pull a stroke that long. The tool may vary depending on the rock, the color of wax, or your pressure; by now, you're learning to have an idea of which tool to use. It is okay if your stroke does not make it all the way to the body, but you should be close.

6.

Pull a curved stroke on the front top wing. Pull it until you meet the body. Pull a curved stroke in the other direction for the bottom of that wing.

7.

Working on the bottom wing, pull a curved stroke up to meet the top wing and body. Pull a stroke to make the bottom part of that wing. See the skipping of the strokes near the tails? I should have varnished the rock a little more to keep this from happening.

8.

In the top wing inside, pull two strokes using an accent color. I used dandelion. Use a smaller tool, and pull the stroke until you reach the body.

9.

Pull a highlight stroke in the bottom wing and in the top, behind the front wing. Of course, if your butterfly is bigger, you could add more strokes to fill the area.

10.

With purple and a little white to lighten it, add descending dots to complete the design.

Think about what type of sealer you want to use on your project. How much will the rock be handled? Will it be in the sun?

I'll spray my rock with Krylon® Triple Thick, or if I want a heavier coat, I'll apply several layers of the brush-on version of Triple Thick.

Once you get the technique down, you will be able to decorate a rock in minutes. Think of all the possibilities. For instance, you could paint the rock with a background color first.

Try a design for fun bugs! See the video at:
http://youtu.be/hEGEkNLAfSU

44

Chapter 6

Putting Wax
on Other Crafts

Paper

You started out by practicing on paper. But, if you pick up the paper and move it around, the wax will pop off. So if you want to create art or designs on paper, choose paper that is thick enough that you cannot bend it.

You can frame a piece of wax artwork that you have done. Another idea is to make color copies of your artwork and use them for cards, or on scrapbooking pages.

You can spice up any picture, from a family photo to a special vacation or occasion, by adding the wax technique to the matting. It makes a great gift. A purchased frame's mat is ready to go; it just needs your special touch or design.

To keep the mat clean while decorating it, spray a light coat of varnish over the mat. Apply a coat of varnish again when you have completed the wax design on the mat. Keep in mind as you work that all photos should be kept out of direct sunlight.

You can also add a wax design to the frame itself, whether it is plastic, wood, or made of something else. Do a test stroke on the back to see how the wax pulls. Seal the frame when done.

There is a video to help you with this project at:
http://youtu.be/aE1PSZfaq8Q

Wood

The wax design technique can be applied to wood. If the wood is not sealed, do a test stroke on the back. If it does not pull smooth, seal or varnish the wood before putting your wax design on. The rougher the wood, the more it may need to be sealed or varnished first. You may have to do a couple coats of varnish if the wood is not sanded smooth. Do a test stroke on the back between coats of varnish.

The decoration-worthy items made of wood are endless. Think about items around the house that are made out of wood and could use a nice design.

Wood stars make great decorations for the home. You can base coat the wood with any color acrylic paint and add the wax design on top. If you want the wood grain to show through, do a color wash on the star. A color wash is acrylic paint watered down, allowing you to apply a thin coat of color. On the blue, white, and red stars, I did a stroke similar to the crashing wave stroke up both sides of the stars, and added descending dots to complete the design.

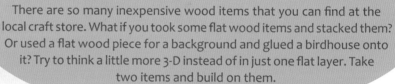

There is a video to help you with this project at:
http://youtu.be/oLDLdLgnODc

Things to Think About...

There are so many inexpensive wood items that you can find at the local craft store. What if you took some flat wood items and stacked them? Or used a flat wood piece for a background and glued a birdhouse onto it? Try to think a little more 3-D instead of in just one flat layer. Take two items and build on them.

Most of us have baskets. Maybe it was a special basket that has been in the family for a long time. Maybe it was a basket that someone special sent you flowers in. If you do not have a basket, you can always find several kinds at the thrift store, usually at a very reasonable price.

When picking out a basket you need to consider your design. A lot of baskets have a band running across the middle, meaning you need a design that can be in two parts.

I fell in love with this basket. I found it on clearance at a craft store. I love the leather around the top and the dark brown color. I could picture little sunflowers on this basket. It has the band near the bottom, so that the design can be in the middle of the basket.

1.

Place little ovals in the center of each section all around the top sections of the basket. These are the centers of the sunflowers. Draw the ovals on with your white charcoal pencil.

5.

Switch back to a smaller wax tool, and pull smaller strokes toward the center stroke on both sides of the leaf. Flip the basket over and repeat on the other side of the flower.

2.

Make sure that you use a color that is light enough to stand out against the dark background. If you had a lighter colored basket you would want darker colors. For this project I used orange crayon. Pull the strokes out away from the center using a small wax tool. Lift the tool up as you pull the stroke to give it a smaller, fatter shape, but bring it to a sharp point. This stroke is like the ones you practiced when making fern leaves. You can do all of the sunflowers or just one sunflower at a time. If using only one melting pot, you'll need to complete all of the sunflowers first.

6.

Add two dandelion descending dots on one side of the flower and one dot on the other side to add a little more brightness to the design. Go back and add brown dots to the inside of the sunflower center.

3.

Dot the center of the sunflower with dandelion descending dots. To keep the dots' shapes do not let them touch each other while warm. After they cool, you can go back and add more dots if you like.

You could sit down and do this project in less than an hour once you are comfortable with the strokes. I love how simple the design is and how much it adds to the basket.
Of course you don't have to stop there. You could add more to the design. You could change the flowers to red for poinsettias for Christmas. Have three or more small flowers and a few small leaves. Do a basket in red, white, and blue for the Fourth of July. Create a basket with pumpkins or leaves for the fall. Fill it with fun stuff and give the basket as a gift.

4.

With a larger tool, pull a yellow-green stroke from each side of the flower. Start at the left side of the section and pull the stroke in to meet the flower in the middle. Flip the basket over and repeat. You will have the strokes curved in opposite directions.

Glass ●●●●●●●●●●●●●●●●●●

Glass is a great thing to add wax designs to. There are so many bottles, vases, glass stones, jars, salt and pepper shakers...and the list keeps going. Bottles come in all shapes and sizes, and also in different colors.

You can add color to bottles or jars with alcohol inks. Clean the glass with rubbing alcohol first. Then brush on the alcohol ink. Once it is dry, heat set it with your embossing tool, then apply your wax design.

Most of my projects start with a trip to the local thrift store or dollar store. When I came across these salt and pepper shakers for a dollar, it got me thinking how cute these would be if decorated. I took them home, washed them, and cleaned the outsides with rubbing alcohol.

1.

With black multisurface acrylic paint, paint two squares on two sides of the shaker. You could use red, blue, or another color if you like to match the color of your kitchen. Use a flat brush that is the width of the square you want. Do not be afraid to take off the paint if you don't like it! Let the paint dry.

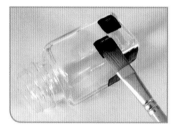

2.

Repeat on the other shaker.

3.

Using the Mini Circle MJ Craft Templates, trace a smaller circle on the open corner; half the flower is on one side and half the flower is on the other side. I traced this with a grease pencil, a good tool for writing on glass.

4.

Add sunflower petals around the circle. Pull a stroke for the center vein of the petal. Refer to chapter 4 where you learned how to create a sunflower. I used dandelion for the color.

5.

Add heart leaves to both sides of the shaker around the sunflower. Or do a different leaf if you like. Remember, you want an odd number of leaves, so do two leaves on one side and one leaf on the other side.

You could reverse the leaves on the other salt shaker or keep them the same.

6.

Add two colors of dots to the center of the sunflower. Keep the dots separate so the wax does not run together, and after they cool, add another layer. Do one layer in dandelion and the other layer in brown.

You could use black instead of brown. You could use orange for a center color to make the flower brighter.

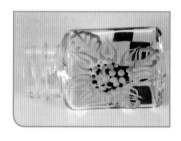

7.

Add descending three dots to fill the open areas and to add to the pattern. I used black, but you could make them other colors to match your décor or someone's favorite color. You might want a stroke with a little curl instead of the descending dots.

Salt and pepper shakers get handled often, so you need to seal them with a good thick sealer, using a few coats. I finished the shakers using marine varnish, dipping each shaker into the marine varnish can up to the bottom of the lid. Once the shaker is finishing dripping, place it on the MJ Dry Board to dry. This varnish has a yellow cast to it which goes well with sunflowers. The shakers need to be wiped by hand, **not washed!**

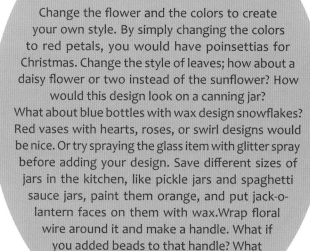

Decorating candles with wax is a great way to give ordinary candles a new look. Adding color with the wax is simple and fun. Flameless candles that are covered with wax to look like real candles can be used as well.

I found a beautiful red, brown, and ivory candle to decorate.

Things to Think About...

Change the flower and the colors to create your own style. By simply changing the colors to red petals, you would have poinsettias for Christmas. Change the style of leaves; how about a daisy flower or two instead of the sunflower? How would this design look on a canning jar? What about blue bottles with wax design snowflakes? Red vases with hearts, roses, or swirl designs would be nice. Or try spraying the glass item with glitter spray before adding your design. Save different sizes of jars in the kitchen, like pickle jars and spaghetti sauce jars, paint them orange, and put jack-o-lantern faces on them with wax. Wrap floral wire around it and make a handle. What if you added beads to that handle? What if you used Mod Podge® and applied colored tissue instead of paint?

1.
I decided to put on a diamond design. I used the square Mini MJ Craft Templates. Place the design in the middle of the candle. The corner of the square template should be on top to make a diamond shape. Pencil or charcoal pencil will not show up on the wax, so as lightly as you can, trace the pattern into the wax. After you're done, you will rub the wax with your finger to remove the line. Put a dot in the center of the diamond so you know where the middle is for your design.

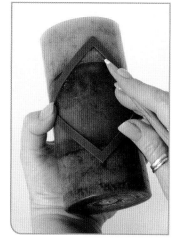

2.

Use the next size down on the square Mini MJ Craft Templates. Turn the candle so the right side corner of the square is facing you. Put the template down so that the corner of the previous square is in the middle of the template. Trace the square from where the last square ended, down to the bottom where it meets up again with the square. Repeat on the left side of the square. From this point on I will call the shapes diamonds because the point is on top.

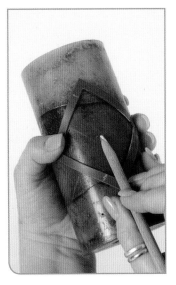

3.

Decide what wax tool is needed for the size of the diamond. With brown wax, start in the four corners, pulling the strokes to the center of the design. Do not worry if the wax does not go all the way to the center; pull the strokes as long as you can toward the center.

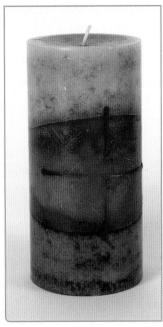

4.

Pull four more strokes in between the first four strokes. Stop if you reach the center of the diamond.

5.

Pull strokes in between the eight other strokes to the center, for a total of sixteen strokes.

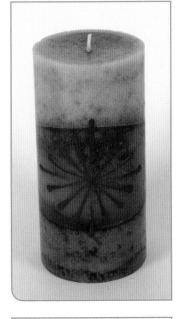

6.

If you have room, pull one more set of strokes in between the previous strokes for a total of thirty-two strokes. Look at the previous picture. See how you can still see through the design at that stage? By adding another set of strokes the design really stands out and does not fade into the background.

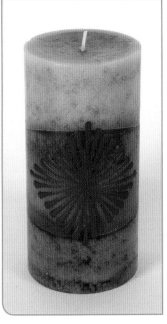

7.

You may want to switch to a smaller tool. Use dandelion crayon for the yellow. Pull a stroke from the three corners toward the middle of this diamond. You do not have the fourth stroke because that is where the other diamond meets up.

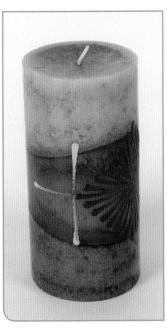

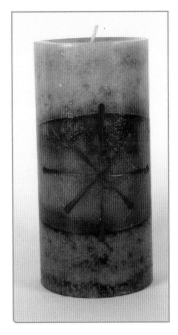

8.

Pull a stroke in between the three strokes you just did. Pull a stroke on each side where the other diamond comes in.

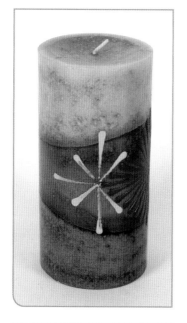

9.

Since you cannot divide the strokes off two more times for a total of three strokes, add two more strokes in between the previous strokes. Repeat on the right side.

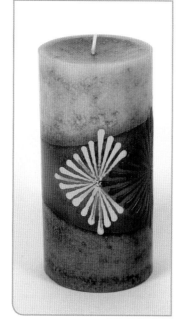

10.

Add dandelion dots around the three tallest strokes in the middle diamond. You can add a dot to the middle of the brown diamond at this time. Switching to red wax, pull a long stroke out from the top where the center diamond meets the one on the left. Moving down following the design, pull a stroke on each side of the one you just did. Repeat on the other top side and both places on the bottom of the design.

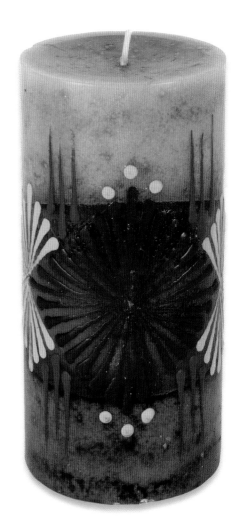

11.

Going back to the brown wax, pull three long strokes above the dandelion dots on both top and bottom of the design. (Leave this step out if it does not fit on your candle.) If you feel the design does not need the red and brown strokes coming out from the design, leave them off. You might like to add more dots instead. What colors do you like? What other designs can you see on the candle?

There is a video to help you with this project at:
http://youtu.be/r7u3neK0n4U

Things to Think About...

What if you made a special candle for a special birthday? How about little daisies on tall, thin candles? What if you painted the candles with some black acrylic paint squares first and then added the flowers?

Tin, Aluminum, and Other Metals • • • • • • • • • •

You can apply wax designs to tin, aluminum and other metals.
Do a test stroke and see how the material pulls.
If the test stroke is not smooth you may need
to seal it first. If the metal is very smooth and
doesn't offer much for the wax to adhere to,
use a heavy sealer or varnish to keep the wax in place.
If the project is flat, you can use epoxy resin.

Make sure that the item you are working on is at room
temperature, not cold. You can heat the item up with a blow
dryer or embossing tool. A cold item will make the wax go on
blotchy.

I found this metal star at a thrift store.

1.

I do not always know the whole
design when I start a project.
I decided to begin with placing
a heart on this star. I drew on
my design with a white charcoal
pencil.

2.

Pull three white
strokes on each side of the
heart. Repeat this design on
all five arms of the star.

3.

The heart needs a little more,
so add a smaller stroke on each
side making a smaller heart.
Repeat the design on all five
arms of the star.

4.

On one side of the star pull
three smaller strokes directly
under the heart, moving toward
the tip of the star. Repeat on
the other side of the star.
Repeat the design on all five
arms of the star.

5.

Use a diamond Mini MJ Craft
Template and trace on half of
the diamond shape at the
center of the star. Trace the
template with the white
charcoal pencil so you can see
the line.

6.

Complete the design all the way to the center of the star to form a smaller star.

7.

Following the pattern, pull strokes from the line in toward the center of the star. You can divide these strokes off to make them more even if you like, or work your way around the star one stroke at a time.

8.

Remove the white charcoal pencil with a damp Magic Eraser. Wipe off the chalky film left behind with a damp paper towel.

9.

Notice how the lines skipped and were not as nice as you would like them to be? If you have a color of paint that matches your wax, you can touch that up. Use white acrylic paint and a liner brush. Water your paint down to an ink consistency. Load your brush and twist it as you are pulling it out of the paint.

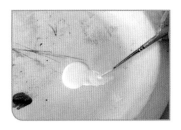

10.

Paint any tails that need cleaned up, or the tail of a stroke that needs to be a little longer.

When you use paint to clean up your strokes or make them longer, remember to make sure your paint matches the color of the crayon wax.

11.

Once you have the star looking the way you want it, seal it with whatever method you choose.

Things to Think About...

What about adding wax to that metal clock that is kind of plain, hanging on your wall? What items can you find at the local thrift store? Don't forget that old saw blade that you found at the antique shop. Metal or tin ceiling tiles are fun to do as well.

There is a video for another fun project at:
http://youtu.be/5H9V2OxgMb0

Eggs ● ● ● ● ● ● ● ● ● ● ● ● ● ● ● ● ● ●

You can use wax design techniques on any type of egg—chicken eggs, ostrich eggs, emu eggs, and so on. We all know where to find chicken eggs. Use the Internet to look for sources of the bigger eggs.

To prepare an egg for a wax design, poke a hole in both ends of the egg and blow out the yolk. This way your egg never goes bad. The egg is still fragile though. Keep in mind that there are some great alternatives nowadays. There are many kinds of craft-material eggs on the market at Easter time. You can also put wax designs on bright colored plastic Easter eggs. These would be more for decoration than use, a basket full of decorated plastic eggs in the center of the table would be pretty. There are also ceramic eggs and egg gourds that you can use in place of a real egg.

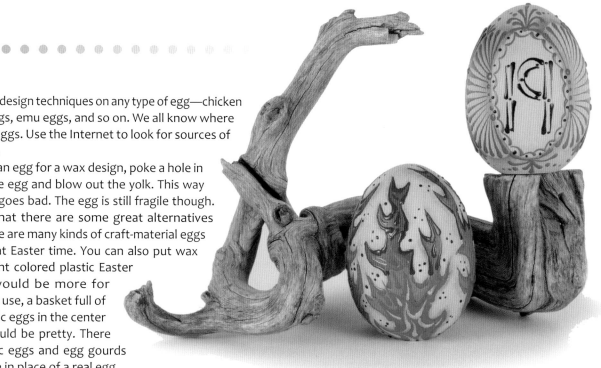

Have your project tell a story. On July 30, 2014, the town where I live, Prescott, Arizona, lost nineteen members of a firefighting crew. Known as hotshots, they were fighting a fire that was threatening a small nearby town. These eggs were found unharmed in a house that had burned to the ground in that town. The eggs were given to local artists to paint and help raise money for the people of the town who had lost their houses in the fire. When I held the eggs in my hand, you could still smell the smoke lingering.

So these eggs are in honor of the nineteen fallen heroes. The eggs will be passed on and a story will be told. What story do you have to tell?

Things to Think About...

You could create a colored background on your eggs with dyes or paint. Try some roses and other flowers you learned how to do in chapter 4. What if you added circle or double circle designs to the eggs? To display and decorate, place your egg on top of a candle holder. Use a couple or more eggs for a centerpiece.

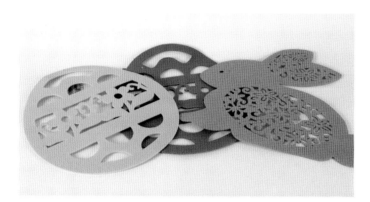

Felt was one of the items I had just not been able to successfully apply wax to. The felt would simply absorb the wax right up. There were so many cute felt cutouts inspiring me, though, that I kept trying to find a way to apply the wax.

I eventually found that if you seal the felt first, then you can pull the wax on the felt. I sealed the felt with two very wet layers of Mod Podge first. Let it dry very well in between coats. Now I was able to apply the wax to the felt. It still absorbs a little. The strokes are not as long but the colored wax really adds so much fun to felt decorations. I just followed the basic design of the felt with the wax. You can use the Mod Podge again over the wax to seal or apply a heavier varnish if need. Just do a text sample to make sure the sealers will work with each other. I put a lot of different varnishes or sealers over other types.

Things to Think About...

Check your local dollar store or craft section during each holiday for different felt designs. Glue rhinestones, pearls, or other embellishments onto the felt to enhance the design. What if you tied a ribbon around the neck of the rabbit, deer, or other animal? What if you used metallic crayons instead of regular crayons? Would that give it a more festive look? What if you glued googly eyes on for a playful piece? Do not glue plastic eyes on with a hot glue gun, it will melt the eyes. Use a low temp or other type of glue.

Know what you are doing when working with felt. You cannot remove unwanted wax without a mess. Know where you are going with the wax. Go around the project with your tool loaded with wax, not over it. So if the wax drips it will not drip on the felt piece. If you do get a drip on the felt, can you work the drip into your design? If not let the wax dry completely and remove as much as possible with your hobby knife.

There is a video to help you with this project at:
http://youtu.be/hzEg-xG2_Ag

Rocks

You already know from your Rock Butterfly (chapter 5) that you can use wax on a rock. When a rock has not been polished you sometimes need to seal it first, for the wax to pull well, but if you are working with a rock that has been cut and polished, the opposite situation happens. The rock's surface is so glass-like that the wax is easy to knock off, so be careful with your strokes and make sure that you put on a thick sealer after you are done with your design.

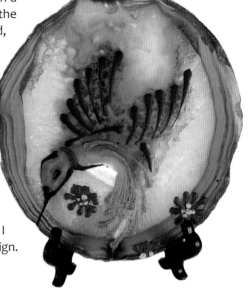

Let the rock tell you what it is. In this slice of agate, do you see the hummingbird?

I simply followed the design in the rock and brought the hummingbird out. I added a few colorful flowers to the design.

1.

Let's try another piece. See the clouds in the sky with the lightning coming out the right side, and the waves of the ocean and shoreline in front? You need a sailboat on the ocean and a lighthouse at the side. Draw these on with a pencil.

2.

Use very small strokes with gray wax to bring out the cloud design that is already in the rock piece. There are two layers in this cloud.

3.

Use white wax to create the sail of a sailboat. Notice how I am using the strokes: larger at the bottom of the sail, pulling them up to the top of the sail.

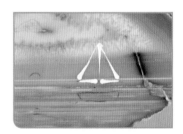

4.

Use brown wax to create the boat itself. Do not draw the bottom of the boat, since it is sitting in the water. Do some strokes to fill in the body of the boat.

5.

Put on some of the blue ocean waves so that you can see how they fit with the body of the boat. (I didn't do the other side, because I want to create a sunset reflecting off the water.)

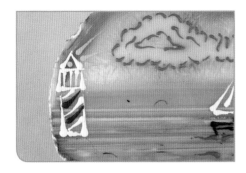

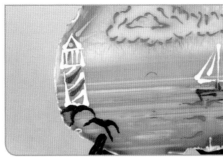

6.

Create the lighthouse with a series of red and white strokes. White strokes to form the outside of the lighthouse. For the middle section of the lighthouse, do white stripes in one direction and red stripes in the other direction. Use a dandelion dot in the lighthouse with outgoing strokes to create the light.

7.

Use black wax strokes to create the rocks the lighthouse sits on. Start the rock from the middle and pull the strokes out each time from the same spot.

8.

With dandelion wax, add the sun by placing a dot and moving the tool a little on the sides of the dot to create a half circle. Using a very small wax tool, pull reflected sunlight strokes across the ocean. The strokes should get bigger the farther away they get from the sun.

10.

With a cotton swab and some rubbing alcohol, very carefully remove any pencil lines and fingerprints. Be careful to avoid the wax.

Since the wax can easily be knocked off this rock's smooth surface, apply an epoxy resin to the agate. Pour the resin over the top of the rock and very carefully move the resin around with a wooden

9.

Now finish the waves, making some strokes through the sun reflection. With a small tool, create the birds by joining two curved strokes with black wax. Finish off the design with lightning done with the wax liner.

craft stick. Shine a light on the piece to see if you have covered the whole front surface of the rock with resin. Make sure to remove any resin drips from the back of the rock. Then let dry. The resin gives the rock a clear coat, and it will be waterproof and sun-proof.

Things to Think About...

What if you did a double circle pattern on a rock and melted the wax a little with the embossing tool? How about if you put designs on several small stones and placed them in a decorated plate to create a centerpiece? Find small stones at the beach, a lake, or just look around you. How about a design on red sandstone?

Boxes •

Whether they are made of cardboard, wood, glass, plastic, or any of the other materials we've discussed in this chapter, boxes offer great opportunities to showcase your wax designs.

1.

On this box I painted only the top surface; the box already had a cute design on the sides. I used a dark purple color that accented its side decorations. Using the square MJ Craft Templates, lay three of the templates inside each other on the top of the box. Trace the inside square with the white charcoal pencil.

2.

While holding down the two outside templates, remove the smallest square, and trace the inside of the larger square with the white charcoal pencil.

3.

Remove the inside square leaving the last square. Trace along the inside of that square.

4.

With white wax, pull a stroke from each of the four corners toward the middle of the box. Let the stroke run out of wax, pulling it as far as you can.

5.

Pull a stroke on each side of the middle stroke to form a fleur-de-lis. The strokes should be down just a little from the first stroke and should curve into the center stroke. Do this on all four corners.

6.

Pull a curved stroke over toward each corner, starting at the center of one side. The stroke should meet the fleur-de-lis in the corner. Repeat this stroke going the other direction to form a heart. Repeat the **design starting at the outermost line and stopping at the inside line.**

7.

Repeat this design on all four sides of the box.

8.

Switch to silver wax and, using the same tool or a larger one, add dots in between where the top and bottom heart meet. Do this at all four sides. Switching to a smaller tool, pull silver strokes from the four corners to the center in the smallest square.

9.

Pull lines in between the strokes again, for a total of eight strokes.

10.

If you have room, divide the space with strokes again for a total of sixteen strokes.

11.

Remember what I said about sometimes not knowing the whole design when you start? Here, notice that you have room to add another row of strokes to the fleurs-de-lis. Starting under the last set of strokes in the corners, pull a smaller stroke on each side of the design filling in that area.

12.

Starting at the center of the hearts next to the silver dot, add white descending dots on each side. Repeat on all four sides. Add a large dot to clean up the tails where they all come together.

13.

Do two descending dots from the top of the inside heart to the silver square on all four sides. Varnish the box at this time.

14.

Glue embellishments on after you have varnished the project. Pearl embellishments, often sold with scrapbooking supplies, work beautifully because they are flat on one side. Use a larger pearl in the middle and smaller ones near the edge of the box. Glue the pearls on with permanent craft adhesive like E6000.

Things to Think About...

To make the box really elegant, line the inside with fabric. What if you applied tissue paper to the box with Mod Podge before adding a wax design to it? Add glitter to the design. Use a bigger stone in the center of the design. Try a masculine design, and add fish lures to the box. Try creating a box using bright colors and attaching plastic zoo animals, dinosaurs, or bugs?

Glittered Items

I saved the best for last! I love to use wax designs on glittered items. Glittered decorations are abundant and inexpensive, and I pick up many of these at dollar stores.

The first thing you should do with an item that is covered in glitter, even if you are not going to put wax on it, is to spray gloss varnish on it. This keeps the glitter on the item for years to come. Otherwise, the glitter is more likely to fall off and the surface underneath becomes exposed.

Since glitter is not smooth it is very hard to remove a stroke, so practice your design on paper first. When you're comfortable with the design and the color of wax you are using (remember, each color is thicker or thinner, so applies a bit differently), apply it to the wax. If you apply an accidental drop of wax as you work, allow it to cool and then see if you can pop most of the wax off with your hobby knife.

1.

With this glitter gift box, you can give that special someone a gift, and make its presentation as wonderful as the present.

2.

Start by marking at least half of a circle using the circle MJ Craft Templates. The size of the template will depend on the size of the box and the size you want your flower to be. This flower has a bigger center.

You want the remaining half of the flower on the other side of the box. Lightly trace the circle on with the white charcoal pencil. You do not want to scratch the glitter.

3.

I used black wax on this design to really make it pop. The flower design here is similar to the cosmos flower, except you are going to add an extra curved stroke on the top of the petal. I used an MJ Wax Design Tool #1, large end. The wax may not pull as far on the glitter as it does on other surfaces.

About half an inch above the half circle, pull a stroke curved and to the right. Stop at the half circle. Now pull a stroke curving to the left, leaving a space in between the two strokes. Start on top of the left stroke and pull it up and over until you meet up with the stroke on the right. You have formed the first petal.

4.

Put petals all around the half circle to form the flower. Leave a little space between the petals. You can do the whole flower at one time, or you can work on one side of the box at a time.

5.

Pull a stroke up from the half circle through the petal. You could do descending dots or small strokes if you like. Take what you've learned from making other flowers and start to build your own style.

6.

Pull strokes from the center of the half circle toward the middle. Place a dot with the white charcoal pencil in the center if you need to, for a reference point. As you can see, I did not make it to the center. You can change to a larger tool if needed.

7.

Place descending dots, varying in size, in the middle of the flower to fill in the space.

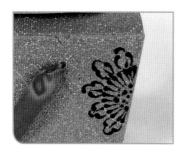

8.

Repeat the flower design on the left side of the box. Then add a fleur-de-lis design (or another design) to fill in the space. I did descending dots at the top of the flower petals as well, to help fill in the area. Or, instead, you could use the grouping of three descending dots here and there.

9.

Trace the half circles on the other sides of the box and continue your flowers. I did the front and back first, and then did the sides of the box. You may find it easier to work around the box.

10.

Use the fleur-de-lis and descending dots to fill in the area between the two designs. You could do a half flower on the bottom of the box if you like, instead of the fleur-de-lis.

11.

Trace the center of the flower on the top tabs on the lid. Keep enough room for the flower petals. Make these flowers smaller, if needed, to fit a whole flower on.

12.

Make the flowers on the lid the same way you did on the sides of the box. Remember to move the tool loaded with wax *around* the box, not over the project, to reach the area you're working on. That way, if you drip, you'll avoid getting the wax on the glittered surface.

13.

Add extra designs to corners and any little extra areas that need to be filled in. You can spray varnish the box or use a brush-on varnish.

How beautiful. The perfect presentation for that special little gift!

Things to Think About...

Use metallic or glitter crayons to give your projects extra sparkle. And don't be afraid to try adding a little glitter in the wax. You'll need to stir the wax more often.

Chapter 7
● ● ● ● ● ● ●

Favorite Projects

In this chapter, you'll learn how to make some of the
most popular wax projects, as well as a few of my
favorites. I'll also introduce you to QuikWood and
how much it can add to a project.

Let's get started!

Decorated Flower Letter · · · · · · · · · · · · · · ·

There are tons of letters to be found out there, in crafts stores, home stores, and even at thrift stores. They come in all shapes and sizes. The letters might be pressed wood, cardboard, or papier-mâché.

1.

Decide what color you want to make the letter. I wanted something bright, and a color the design would show up well on. I painted the letter with crocus-yellow acrylic paint.

It can take several coats to base coat bright yellow paint. It works better if you start with a straw yellow, which is thicker. Let that dry then apply two coats of the bright yellow.

2.

Don't worry if you can't think of the whole design at this point. Start out in the fattest part or middle of the letter, and draw a small design. I used small cosmos flowers. Use an odd number of petals.

3.

Pick your palette for the project. I picked robin's egg, carnation pink, orange, yellow-green, and purple with a little white added to lighten it. Hold the colors you've chosen together, making sure you are looking at the wax of the crayon, not the wrapper.

Make sure they all coordinate and that you like the colors.

I put a flower behind the other two flowers. Do not worry if you are not sticking to the sketched pattern. The pattern is just an idea.

4.

Add another flower if you feel it is needed. By doing them in different colors, you can see each individual flower nicely. Use leaves to fill in open areas. I started with a long stroke down the middle and did smaller strokes on each side of the center stroke.

5.

Start with big strokes, slightly curved, and put smaller strokes on one side of the leaf to create the leaves. This gives it an airy feeling. You can put one or two curved strokes on the inside of the leaf. Start with bigger strokes at the bottom of the

leaf, moving to the smallest strokes at the top of the leaf. Start with a larger wax tool and move to the smallest of your wax tools.

6.

Put some larger flowers onto the letter. Start by tracing the inside of a circle MJ Craft Template to form the center of the flower. You only want a little of the flower's center on the letter so that most of the design will be petals.

7.

Use an orange crayon to create the circle design for the inside of the flower. Pull the strokes off the sides when you run out of room.

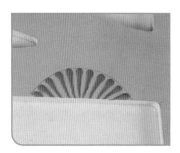

8.

Do the cosmos flower, with descending dots added to it this time. This helps fill up the design and gives it a different look.

9.

Put two more of the bigger cosmos flowers on the letter. Each time, do something a little different to the flower. You can do a stroke in between the petals or do dots in the center instead of the circle design.

10.

Attach leaves to the big flowers. Start from the area you need to fill in. Have a couple of leaves attached to the first leaf to fill in the area until you get to the flower. Make sure to curve the leaf so you are going from one side of the letter to the other side.

11.

Use the same color for the center of the little flowers as you used for the big ones. Use a smaller tool to make the smaller dots.

12.

If your letter is one that has a straight line across, decorate that with wax by doing one stroke up and one stroke down. The tool needed will depend on the size of the area. I had two of these on my letter M. You can also use this method to do the whole letter if you want. It works well on smaller letters too.

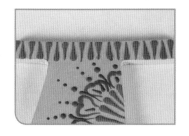

13.

Fill in the rest of the letter with little flowers and leaves. Make sure that you have little flowers in all the curves of the letter. Do some single flowers in the smaller areas. Complete the design by adding descending dots in orange to fill in and bring the designs together.

14.

Decide what type of sealer you want. If the letter is going to be in a kid's room you may want to use epoxy resin, which provides a very sturdy finish.

This is another project inspiration I found in a dollar store. I saw the possibilities but never imagined how beautiful these masks would turn out.

There was already cording around this mask but you could replace that edging with something else. For a really elegant mask, you could use flat pearl or rhinestone strands (usually sold with scrapbooking supplies) rather than beading supplies, because they are flat on one side and will glue onto your mask easily.

The first thing I did was to spray gloss varnish on the mask to seal the glitter. (You should spray any glitter item with varnish to keep the glitter on the item.)

I created the first mask using metallic crayons, in the colors metallic sunburst and metallic seaweed. I knew instantly that this was going to be a favorite.

I am not going to walk you through this project step by step, because instead I want you to start thinking of how you would create a design. I am going to point out how I started and lead you through sections, so you know how to start and where to go from there.

Start around the eye holes. The main focus of a mask is the eye holes or the eyes of a person wearing it. For the pink mask, I just pulled blue strokes around the eye holes to bring them forward and form an eye shape.

On the black mask I did the crashing wave design around the top of the eye holes. This makes the eyes very dramatic. I thought it would be too much to do it on the bottom as well. The wax is silver crayon.

Metallic seaweed was the second color I used on the mask. I completed the eyes by adding strokes below them. Next I started working in the middle top of the mask. You can use a type of fleur-de-lis design or any design you think it calls for. Next I added wax designs to the top sides of the mask. Include some straight strokes and some curved. The curved strokes give the mask more of an elegant feel.

Add wax designs to the bottom sides of the mask. Start under the outside end of the eye hole and work your way back to the side of the mask. You may need to add some designs to fill in the bottom edge of the mask's nose. Add dots and descending dots to clean up and fill in empty areas. Switch colors for the dots; if you did a silver design put seaweed dots in.

After I varnished my mask, I glued butterfly embellishments over the ribbon holes. On other masks I've added pearl beads in the middle of the cording. I have also added pearls or rhinestones in place of some of the dots. Glue them on with permanent craft adhesive like E6000.

To complete these masks and really dress them up, I glued on feathers. For the black mask I found some little black feathers with beads already attached to a circle felt base.

I glued it on my mask and was done. Simple! **Remember that if you use a glue gun it must be on low setting so you do not melt your wax.**

For the pink mask I found feathers that were already sewn into fabric. I then glued the pink feathers on the front of those feathers, and added a peacock feather on the bottom. I then glued the feather decoration onto the mask. If you are working with feathers that don't have a fabric or base, it is easier to glue them onto a felt or fabric base than to try to glue them, loose, directly onto the mask.

Things to Think About...

I think every teenage girl goes through the "decorated mask" phase. What a wonderful thing to make, or help them make, for their room. If you plan to use your masks for wall decoration, I suggest making two. The price is right, and with more than one mask you can also expand your color use to creatively match a room.

Gold Sunburst Frame ● ● ● ● ● ● ● ●

One of the most popular things to embellish with wax—and definitely one of my favorites—is wooden picture frames. You can pick these up at a dollar store or at craft stores in the section with the unfinished wood items. A frame is a wonderful present for a friend or family member. Include a photo that captures special memories of them!

1.

Start by watering the red acrylic paint down with just a little water to make a nice bright wash. This allows the wood grain to show a little, and you do not have to do several layers of paint to base coat the project. Put your paint on with a paint brush. Allow to dry.

Dip your craft sea sponge into water. Squeeze the sponge out until there is no water coming out of the sponge. If you leave the sponge too wet, the paint will bleed and not leave a nice sponged design. Pour some gold metallic acrylic paint onto a plate. Pull the paint out from the edge and pounce your sponge into the pulled paint, not the main pool of paint. This keeps you from getting globs of paint on your project. Pounce the sponge on the plate or a piece of paper until you get a nice even design. Then move over to the frame and pounce gold paint onto the frame.

2.

Make sure to move the sponge around so that the design is varied. Once you have completed the gold metallic color, rinse out your sponge and repeat with bronze metallic paint and amethyst (purple) metallic paint. Allow the paint to dry between each color.

3.

Using the circle Mini MJ Craft Templates, stack a few together, one inside of another. The largest template should be half on the frame with enough room for some dots on the top of the design. Then add templates to the center until you have the small circle size that you want in the half center. Trace the inside of the smallest circle with a white charcoal pencil.

4.

Still holding the outside template in place, remove the inside templates. Trace the inside of the largest template. (Remember that if the white charcoal pencil does not write smoothly, you can heat its tip with a flame.)

5.

You can write on the templates with the white charcoal pencil, to mark where the template needs to line up with the frame.

6.

Mark the same circle design on all four sides of the frame. Along the center edge, place a mark at the center of the half circle; it will show you where to end your wax strokes.

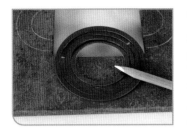

7.

In this design you will be creating half of the basic double circle design from chapter 4. Start with a large tool, and begin on the outside circle. This will keep the smaller strokes on top, and the strokes will be neater because you will not be trying to pull the larger strokes in between the smaller strokes.

Pull the first stroke, using metallic sunburst, from the top middle of the second circle to the middle of the circles. It's okay to pull the stroke off the edge of the frame. Pull a stroke on the left, next to the bottom of the frame, to the center of the circle. Repeat on the right side.

8.

Pull strokes in the area between the strokes you just did, one on each side.

9.

Again pull strokes in between each of the strokes you just did, for a total of nine strokes. Repeat on the opposite side of the frame.

10.

On the other two sides of the frame, complete the same steps as above. On these designs, add one more set of strokes in between, for a total of thirteen strokes.

11.

Starting on the inside circle, add brown wax strokes in between the gold strokes. You will have more brown strokes on the second set of two half circles because they have more gold strokes. Use a smaller tool.

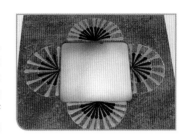

12.

Make sure you are pulling all of the half circles to the middle dot you marked along the inside edge of the frame. This keeps the design neat and clean.

13.

Take the Magic Eraser and remove all of the white charcoal pencil lines. It is easier to do this now when there are not any wax dots to work around. Wipe with a damp paper towel to remove the chalky film.

14.

Use the same size tool as you did for the gold strokes. Make your turquoise color by mixing equal parts of blue-green and white crayons. Stir well until the wax becomes one solid color. Working on a half circle

with nine strokes, add descending dots going out, beginning just above the brown strokes. Repeat on the other nine-stroke half circle.

15.

On a thirteen-stroke half circle, add a single dot just above and in between the gold strokes. Make sure you are reloading for each dot to keep them consistent in size. Repeat on the last half circle.

16.

Switch back to the smaller wax tool. Pull a brown stroke down in the four corners. Pull a stroke just a little down on each side of the first stroke. Pull one more on each side if you have room. This is similar to the fleur-de-lis design.

17.

Using the turquoise color add three dots, starting at the center brown stroke. Do this on all four corners. This completes your wax design.

Adding Dimension with QuikWood

To really add dimension to your frame, or to other projects, you can add QuikWood to it. QuikWood is a product used for wood repairs. Anything you do to wood you can do to QuikWood: sand it, seal it, paint and drill it. I treat it like clay. What I love about QuikWood is that it allows you thirty minutes of working time, yet it is rock hard in an hour.

I will be calling the QuikWood epoxy "clay" below, because that is how I use it.

1.

The first step when working with QuikWood is to remove all of your jewelry. Because rock hard means rock hard, even if it's in your jewelry.

4.

Spread the spray around with your finger to make sure that it coats all the corners.

2.

Spray your hand with a vegetable spray. This keeps the QuikWood from sticking to your hands.

5.

Take the QuikWood out of its container. Read all the manufacturer's precautions. Remove the foil circle from the top of the roll.

3.

Spray the inside of the mold too. I used a mold that I found in the jewelry section of the craft store. The mold has fleurs-de-lis and shell-looking fleurs-de-lis on it. There are many molds you can use. Check different sections of the craft store. You can use cake molds, candy molds, clay molds, jewelry molds...any type of mold that is flexible will be easy to use.

6.

QuikWood is a two-part epoxy. It is premeasured. All you have to do is mix it to activate it. You can see the equal parts here. One is tan and the other part is white.

7.

Using scissors, cut the amount needed to fill your mold piece. It is better to have too little than too much; you can always add more if you run out. Place the foil circle back on top of the roll to help keep it fresh. (If you are done with the QuikWood, put it back into the plastic container and put the lid on.)

8.

A plastic wrap covers the roll of QuikWood. Don't remove it from the roll; instead, you will remove it from each small piece you cut. This keeps the rest of the QuikWood fresh. You do have to remember to remove the plastic off the smaller piece! I cannot tell you how many times people forget and can't figure out what's wrong with the epoxy, until they notice there is a piece of plastic in it.

9.

Knead the two parts together to activate the QuikWood. This step is very important. If you forget to knead it together or do not knead it enough, the epoxy will not harden.

10.

Knead until all the marbling is gone and it becomes one solid color. It will start to become warm to the touch.

11.

Begin pressing the clay into the mold. Push it around to fill the whole area.

12.

The clay should not be mounded above the mold. Take your thumb and slide it across the top of the mold, removing any clay that sticks out. If you have extra clay, cover it with wax paper and save it. You can add it to the next batch of clay for the next mold as long as it is not starting to get hard.

13.

Position the mold above the place you want the design to go, in this case the very corner of the frame. Push on the mold with your thumb. Make sure you push on the entire mold— don't leave out the edges. This will help the clay unmold onto the frame. Check to see whether the clay design is sticking to the frame; if not, push on the mold a little harder.

14.

This gets easier with practice. If you don't like the design that you just did, take it off and try again. Roll it back into a ball and put it back in the mold. Remove any clay from the frame and try again.

15.

You may have clay that squished out the sides of the mold. If you have a little clay outside the mold design, take your hobby knife and use it around the edges to clean up the design.

If there is a lot, remove the design and redo it, using less clay in the mold; also make sure you don't have extra clay mounded above the mold.

16.

Place the clay design on all four of the corners of the frame.

18.

Brush the gold pigment powder onto the clay design. Because the clay is still wet, brush lightly to avoid disturbing it.

17.

While the clay is wet, it is still sticky. Before the corner clay designs start to harden, apply some gold pigment powder. (Pigment powder is found in the scrapbooking supplies sections of craft stores, with

embossing powders.) With a mop brush, dip into the powder. Set your brush into the lid and tap off excess powder. Never go straight from the bottle to your project; there is too much powder on the brush, and it will just make a mess.

19.

Make sure you apply pigment to the side edges of the design. Let the QuikWood dry.

20.

Remove any stray gold pigment powder from the frame with a damp cotton swab. I like to leave a little around the design. It gives it a bit of a shadow.

21.

Decide how you want to seal the frame. It is flat, so you can use epoxy resin or triple-thick brush-on. I used marine varnish for this project. It gave it a heavy coat and covered all the dots and clay. After your sealant is dry, glue on the embellishments with permanent craft adhesive like E6000.

Things to Think About...

Now that you know how to add QuikWood to your wax project to give it a dimensional look, what clay design shapes and styles would you like to put on a frame? What kinds of frames can you find to decorate? What other colors of wax would you choose to totally change the design?

There is a video to help you with this project at:
http://youtu.be/y44vzaxqwkE

This next project has a romantic feel to it. A soft pink color and a lovely rose, together with the bold design of black wax...I can see it sitting on the dresser of someone special, anyone from a little girl to your grandmother. I paid a dollar for this papier-mâché round box at the craft store. There are usually lots of box shapes to choose from!

In the last project you learned how to work with QuikWood and use it in a mold. In this project, we will shape it by hand. Make sure that you have read through the steps for making the Gold Sunburst Frame project above, in particular, the instructions on how to prepare the QuikWood and your hands. As a reminder, I will be calling the QuikWood "clay" because that is how I use it.

1.

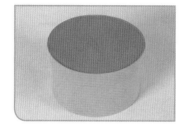

Start with a papier-mâché round box. Paint the box with pink acrylic paint. Use at least two coats of pink to get an even layer of paint. (How many coats of paint you need varies depending on the color of acrylic paint. You have applied enough coats of paint when the paint looks even and you see no spots or blotches.)

Make sure to paint the entire box. Nothing looks more incomplete then a box with the back or inside unpainted. You can always add a liner inside the box to make it look even more elegant.

2.

Using a large wax tool, pull black strokes to form the rolling wave design around the lid. Draw the basic pattern on with the white charcoal pencil if you are not comfortable freehanding the design. I used black as my color. It makes the piece more dramatic. You may like a different color of wax.

3.

Going the opposite direction, add the rolling wax design to the bottom of the box. Keep the strokes the same size as the design on the top lid.

4.

Add the design around the top of the lid. Do you like the design running in one direction better than in the other? Try to keep these strokes the same size as the strokes on the side of the box.

5.

Of course the design is not complete without dots. Add dots to both sides of the design on the lid. Remember that you need to load your tool for each dot to keep them the same size.

6.

On the top side strokes, add the dots to the top of the rolling wave design. On the bottom strokes, add the dots to the bottom of the rolling wave design. You have now completed the wax part of this project. It's a small part but adds so much.

7.

Working with a small amount of QuikWood, form a cone-like shape. You want it to come to a rounded, not a sharp, point on top. This is the middle of our rose.

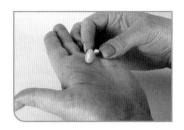

8.

You will be using yellow-green, pink, and gold pigment powders for this project. Take your mop brush and dip into the pink to pick up the powder. Knock off the excess powder in the lid then lightly paint the

middle of the clay piece. If you have another mop brush, dip it into the gold pigment and lightly add a little gold on the very top of the piece. If you don't have a second brush, just rub the pink out on a paper towel before you dip into the gold pigment.

9.

To form the first petal of the rose, roll a ball of clay in the middle of your hand. Squish the clay flat with your finger to form a petal. If you do not like the shape, you can just roll it into a ball and start again!

The petal should be narrower at its base and wider as it lengthens. Start with smaller balls of clay for these first, centermost petals.

10.

With your mop brush, apply the pink pigment powder to the petal while it is still in your hand. Do not worry about painting the back at this point. Putting the pigment powder on now, instead of after you

add it to the rose, helps maintain the shape of the rose.

11.

Add gold pigment powder to the very top of the petal to give the petal reflective light. Don't worry about the back side yet.

12.

Very gently pick the petal up off your hand and place it around a third of the rose center. Press the petal on at the bottom, leaving the petal turned out. (These photos omit the color to allow you to see the petals better.)

13.

Form your second petal, apply the pigment powder, and attach it to the rose. Place it to overlap the first petal just a little bit.

14.

Form and put pigment powder on your third petal and attach it to the remaining open area on the rose. It should meet the petals on both sides. Lightly press the petal on at the bottom. The tops of the petals should be turned out.

15.

Now paint the backs of the rose petals with pink pigment powder. Redo the gold on the tops of the petals if needed. If during your pigmenting you pushed the top of any petal too far inward, pull it back away

from the center just a little. The petals near the center should be closer to the center piece. You will pull each set of petals out a little farther than the last as you work toward the outside of the rose.

Gently set the rose on a piece of wax paper that's been sprayed with a little vegetable spray so the rose will not stick to the paper. Now let the rose harden. If you were to continue to work on the rose and keep adding petals at this point, you'd lose the shape of the inside petals. Allow thirty to forty-five minutes of hardening time. When the rose is hard to the touch, continue on.

16.

Add a new layer of petals in the same way as the first layer. Start in between the petals on the first row. Pull each of the new petals back a little farther from the center.

17.

You will add one more petal to this layer than you did in the layer before it. The second layer has four petals.

Stop and let the petals dry in between each layer so that your rose does not turn into a ball of mush. Waiting is so hard, but it is worth it.

18.

Add more petals that are larger in size. The tops of the petals should be turned more outward. Start the layer in between the petals on the last layer.

19.

Add pink pigment to the backs of the petals after you complete each layer. You need to do this while the clay is still wet and sticky.

20.

You may have to touch up the gold on the top edges of the petals. Continue adding rows of petals and letting each layer dry before continuing on to the next row. Make sure that you add one extra petal to each layer. Stop when you like the size of the rose.

21.

Cut off a slightly bigger section of clay to make the leaf. Knead the clay until it's ready, and roll it into a ball.

22.

Roll the bottom of the ball with your finger and form a point at the top. It should be similar to a rounded cone shape.

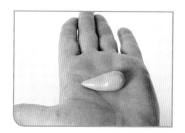

23.

With your finger, push the clay piece flat, forming a leaf shape.

24.

Pull the top of the leaf to a sharp point.

25.

Color the entire leaf with yellow-green pigment powder. You do not have to worry about the back because it will be covered.

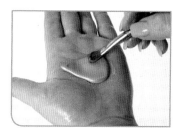

26.

Add reflective light by applying the gold pigment powder around the edges of the leaf and down the center of the leaf. Just a little, not too much; you don't want to overpower the green.

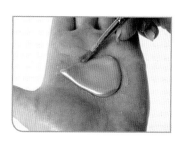

27.

Peel the leaf off of your hand and place it near the center of the box lid. Its tip should nearly reach the wax design but not cover it up. The box lid's center should have enough room left for two more leaves.

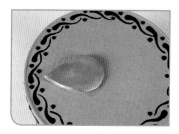

28.

With a clay tool, the side of a credit card, or a similar item, press a middle vein into the center of the leaf.

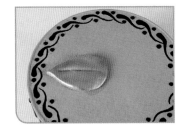

29.

Press to make veins along the center vein, coming out toward the side. Press down deeper near the center and more lightly near the outside edge of the leaf. Repeat on the other side of the vein.

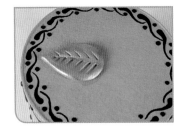

30.

Add two more leaves, made in the same way, to the top of the box. I spaced these equally, but you could place two leaves on one side, overlapping each other, and one leaf on the other side. Just make sure you have an odd number of leaves.

31.

Make sure that your rose is dry. (The leaves can still be wet.) Add a small piece of moist clay to the bottom of the rose and press it down onto the leaves. Make sure that you have not varnished this area of the lid, so that the surface will allow the clay to adhere. If you have varnished the box, or if you simply want to make sure that the clay decoration will stay securely attached, you may put a little craft adhesive like E6000 on the area before you place the clay.

32.

Varnish the entire box including the rose. Spray varnish the rose first if you choose to use a brush-on varnish; this will help keep the pigment powder on the rose. Varnish the inside of the box also. Don't put the lid on your box until the varnish is dry.

There is a video to help you with this project at:
http://youtu.be/u8a_LxYvkbo

Chapter 8

Twice-Melted Wax

Warning!

It's easy to spend hours doing the twice-melted wax technique! It is different every time you do it. Heating the wax gives it a great marbleizing effect.
When working with twice-melted wax, always work on a tray covered with a layer of paper towels to keep the area clean and absorb any melted wax drips or splatters.
Make sure you have your apron on!

Colorful Tile Magnet •••••••••••••••••••

1.

Let's start with a simple project to get the feel for the twice-melted wax technique. Use a 2-inch-by-2-inch ceramic tile that is not sealed. Load your melting pot with your crayons. With the MJ Wax Brush dip the brush into metallic sonic silver. Brush on a little wax. It gives the project its "sparkle" but is dull in color.

2.

You can use any colors you want. The next color I used was red. Use a different brush for each color. They are inexpensive and you don't have to worry about cleaning the brush out. Put on as much red wax as you like. Leave enough room for a couple more colors. **Do not go over warm wax with your brush.** Wait for the wax to harden and then go over it. When the wax is warm you move it around forming ridges. It is harder to melt more evenly.

3.

The next color that I used was robin's egg. (You can also make a turquoise color by mixing blue-green and white half and half. The blue-green is found in the 24 pack of crayons.) Apply it here and there on the tile using your wax brush.

4.

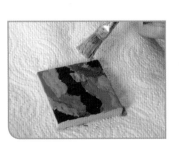

The last color on this tile is dandelion. Dandelion makes the tile "pop." This color brings your art to life! Make sure that you have covered the entire square with wax.

5.

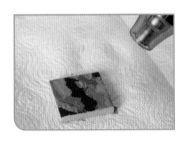

Once all the wax is applied, begin to heat the tile with the embossing tool. Start around the edges and work your way toward the middle. Keep the embossing tool about three to four inches away from the tile.

6.

When the wax starts to warm, also warm your Wax Design Tool #0. The tool has to be warm to move the wax around. Stick it in front of the embossing tool to warm it, or if you have an empty melting pot, you can place it in that well to keep it warm.

7.

With your warm tool, start at the top of the tile and pull down toward you. It is easier to pull the wax toward you.

8.

You know the wax is not warm enough if you can see ridges in the strokes that you just pulled. If there are ridges, just heat the wax until the ridges melt together.

9.

The wax should look "melted" and shiny in color when it is warm enough. The layers of the wax should be melted into one nice even coat. Do not overheat it; the more you heat the wax, the more the colors will mix together and create a mess. Pull lines down the project in any direction you want them to go. You can turn the tile to pull lines from the other side as well.

10.

Sometimes less is better. Do not add too many lines. You may find that you like the tile better with the wax simply melted and not pulled with a tool. You can move the wax around by blowing it with the embossing tool; if you want it to move to one side, heat it on that side. Move the wax around until you like it. If you don't like it, while it is warm, wipe the wax off on a paper towel to start again.

11.

Scrape the wax off the sides of the tile with your hobby knife. Pick a color of acrylic paint that coordinates with the wax on the tile and paint the sides of the tile. I then use at least three layers of triple-thick brush-on to seal the tile. The tile will get handled a lot and fall off the fridge, so you want it to be sturdy.

Once the tile is completely dry, glue on a heavy-duty magnet using permanent craft adhesive like E6000. Let the glue dry for twenty-four hours.

Things to Think About...

Make a set of magnets for a gift. Would it add something if you added glitter to the wax? Use colors to match a party's decor, a business's logo, or a holiday's theme. Send a magnet with your holiday photo cards to use for displaying the card on the fridge.

•••• • Rainbow Earring Holder

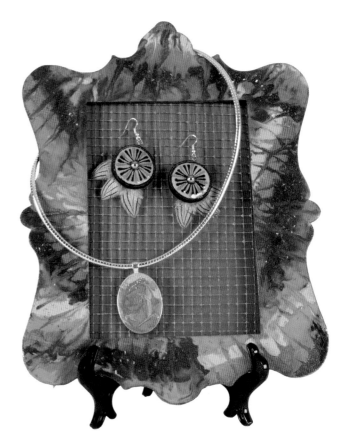

1.

Start with a wooden frame like those that you can find at the craft store. There are lots of styles to choose from.

The wood absorbs the wax when you warm it, so first seal the wood with a wood sealer or varnish. This keeps the wax on the surface, and you use less.

2.

Before you apply the wax to the front, base coat the back of the frame with black acrylic paint or a dark color of your choice. You can base coat the sides of the frame as well, or apply wax to the sides of the frame in a dark color that you are using on the front as well. I used metallic cyber grape. Be sure to coat all four sides of the frame.

3.

You can start with any color you like. I used metallic cyber grape. With the wax brush, start to brush stripes of wax onto the frame. Try to keep the wax fairly thick. If you start to run out of wax, stop and

reload, then start again where you ran out of wax so it is one solid color. Add stripes of wax all the way around the frame with this color. Make sure to go in a different directions with the wax stripes so they are not in even rows, unless that is your chosen design.

4.

Once you have applied the first color, switch to your next color. Apply it right beside the first color so that there are no uncovered spots on the frame. I used carnation pink. Remember not to go over warm wax

with your brush. Wait until it is cool and then apply the wax again.

5.

Start your third color. If you get near an edge of the frame make sure to cover it well with wax. I used robin's egg for this color. Do not worry if the wax looks messy. Have a general idea of how many colors you

are going to put on so that you can allow space for each color.

6.

To make the design "pop" you should bring in a bright lighter color. I used dandelion. When selecting your colors for a project, put the crayons you are choosing all together in your hand to see if the colors all work well together.

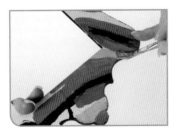

7.

The last color is yellow-green. Fill in any empty areas still left on the frame, but keep in mind that you do not want more yellow-green than any other color. To keep the color use about the same, you may decide

to fill some of that remaining area in with a previous color.

8.

Make sure the frame is entirely covered with wax. Fill in any bare areas that are left. Do not worry about the wax looking good or even at this time. Make sure the lines are not so fine that the wax will mix together

when melted and give you a brown or black wax color. The lines should be at least as wide as your brush.

9.

Set your frame inside a tray covered with paper towels to absorb the drips. You can only control one section of wax at a time, so heat the frame a section at a time. A two-inch strip works well.

10.

Heat the wax tool. To move more of the wax around, use a larger wax tool. If you want smaller lines, use a smaller tool. I used the MJ Wax Design Tool #2.

11.

Once the tool is warm, rewarm the wax area until melted and pull the wax in the area you have heated. If you notice that the wax is absorbing into the wood and not moving around much, add another layer of wax all over the frame.

12.

Continue to work around the frame. The wax next to your previous section is already starting to warm, so it does not take the new section as long to melt.

13.

Pull the wax any direction you want it to go. I pulled mine from the outside of the frame toward the middle of the frame. Once you have an area the way you want it, stop heating that area.

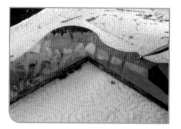

14.

If you notice that the wax is not pulling as smoothly, stop and rewarm your tool. The need for this may vary depending on how hot or cold it is in your work area, and also on any fans or breezes, warm or cold, that may be blowing on the wax.

15.

I find it easier to hold my embossing tool with my left hand, because I am right handed, and pull the wax with the wax tool in my right hand. I can then work better without giving the wax time to cool off and start to harden. If you cannot do that, heat a section at a time with the embossing tool, stop, pull the wax with the wax tool, and repeat.

16.

You can also switch to a smaller tool for areas where you may want the lines to be thinner. Experiment and find what you like. I switched to the Wax Tool #1 for this area.

17.

Add glitter to the wax to add sparkle and fun. I used purple tinsel glitter. I like the bigger, longer style of this glitter.

18.

Heat the wax just a little until it is warm and then apply the glitter. Pick up a little glitter in your fingertips and spread it onto the warm wax. You have better control of the glitter with your fingertips than if you tried to shake it out of the bottle.

19.

After you have applied the glitter, heat the wax just a little more to set it. If the wax hadn't been warmed enough in the last step, the glitter would blow away at this time.

20.

Apply the purple tinsel glitter to the purple wax only. You want your design to stand out, not get lost in a bunch of glitter.

21.

If you like, pick another color and add fine white glitter to that color. A little goes a long way. I applied the fine white glitter to the yellow-green areas.

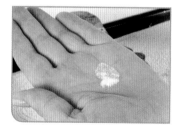

22.

The glitter additions make the frame more fun!

23.

Since this is an item that is going to get handled, seal it with several layers of triple-thick brush-on. Let it dry.

Glue wire mesh on the back of the frame using permanent craft adhesive like E6000. Look for the mesh at your hardware store, feed store, or from vendors online. If you like, you can glue a strip of fabric along the sides to cover the mesh's sharp edges. Just make sure that the fabric can't be seen from the front of your frame.

24.

Set the frame on an easel, or attach a wire on the back to hang it on the wall.

Things to Think About...

There are bigger wooden frames that you could turn into wall mirrors. What other types of embellishments could you glue onto your frames? Now that you have learned how to apply twice-melted wax, what new ideas do you have? What do you want to try it on next? In my book Wax on Crafts Holiday Projects, I show how to use twice-melted wax to make jewelry!

Blue Wave Necklace

Another way to use twice-melted wax is as a filler.

1.

This necklace begins with a shell with a big hole in it. Start the necklace by gluing small colored shell pieces onto the large shell. The shell pieces are used as fillers for vases; find them online or in your craft store in the floral section.

2.

Decide, based on your design, where on the shell you want to adhere your first shell pieces. Apply a light, solid layer of permanent craft adhesive like E6000 to that section of the shell. Pour some of the shell pieces out so you can easily see the different sizes, and use tweezers to pick up shell pieces and place them into the glue. Make sure the shell pieces do not stick outside the big shell. Place the shell pieces in as if you were doing a puzzle, leaving just a tiny space between each piece. It's kind of like applying tile, with grout lines in between. Do not worry about the pieces fitting exactly.

As the glue dries or you complete a section, add more glue down on a new section and continue to work until you have the design you want. I did not cover the entire shell; I wanted it to look like crashing waves, and also, the large shell is so pretty I wanted it to show. Using your hobby knife, remove any glue that is visible. Allow the glue to dry for twenty-four hours.

3.

You already have color due to the shell pieces, so I like to add sparkle using metallic crayons. I used metallic steel blue for this project. Heat the wax in the melting pot. Heat your glass eyedropper in the well of the melting pot. Squeeze the wax up into the tube part of the eyedropper only. Start to fill in all the cracks between your shell pieces.

4.

The wax should be warm enough to flow down into the cracks. Make sure to apply wax all the way around the colored shell pieces, including the edges and top. The colored shell pieces will have different

thicknesses, but the wax should rise a little above them.

5.

With your embossing tool, start to heat the wax, working on one section at a time. Do not overheat the wax; you don't want it so warm that it melts off the shell. You can always heat it more later.

6.

With a clean paper towel, wipe the wax off the top of the shell pieces. This leaves the wax in between the shell pieces. Heat and wipe the next section, and repeat until you have completed the entire area.

7.

Do another round of heating and wiping until you have removed all of the wax on top of the shell pieces. Make sure you also remove the wax on any pieces that are lower than other pieces. The wax should be in the cracks only.

8.

Heat the entire area again just until it is warm enough that you can apply glitter.

There is a video to help you with this project at:
http://youtu.be/dPbmj_lr7Al

9.

For this project I really like using micro beads as glitter. It gives the necklace an ocean feel. Pick a color of micro beads that will accent the colors of your shell pieces and wax. I used silver micro beads.

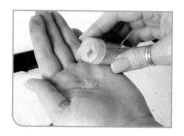

10.

While the wax is still warm, sprinkle the micro beads onto the wax. Some beads will land on the shell pieces. Pick up the pendant and move it from side to side to roll the beads into the wax. You can warm the

wax one more time to set the beads into the wax a little more.

11.

Seal the wax and shell pieces. I didn't apply any sealer to the top part of the shell that has no wax. Make sure to get the edges. To seal the wax and colored shell pieces, I brushed on several layers of 3D Crystal

Lacquer®. You could also use Dimensional Magic to cover the wax. You need to make sure that the wax is completely covered, so that if the necklace is worn on a hot sunny day it will not melt. (The best way to make sure you have the necklace well sealed is to do a test: place it in the hot sun.)

12.

Once the sealer is dry, complete your necklace using chain, cording, or ribbon.

83

Try different colors to change the look. How about an American flag design for the 4th of July?

There is a video to help you with this project at:
http://youtu.be/HzlGZLkTYNc

Sometimes you're lucky and you get a pearl-like shell in your package of shell pieces. You can also make good use of a plastic figure, like this turtle from the dollar store. Put wax on the turtle with a wax brush and melt the wax. Add that to your colored shell design.

There is a video to help you with this project at:
http://youtu.be/lAmLhTln8xk

Use wax to make colored shell piece designs on other items, too. For the blue butterfly vase I started at the bottom of the vase and worked up to create designs with the shell pieces. The pink dragonfly vase features a band of colored stones around the middle. I glued ornaments to the shell-covered areas with permanent craft adhesive.

There is a video to help you with this project at:
http://youtu.be/PoVH6DlOnqE

Things to Think About...

You can use a wood circle or metal piece as your backing for the shell pieces. I used circle gourd pieces as my base for most of these necklaces. The base will determine how the wax will melt; for example, a wood-base pendant will absorb the wax a little and take longer to heat and cool. A metal base will heat and cool the wax faster.

Chapter 9

Advanced Projects

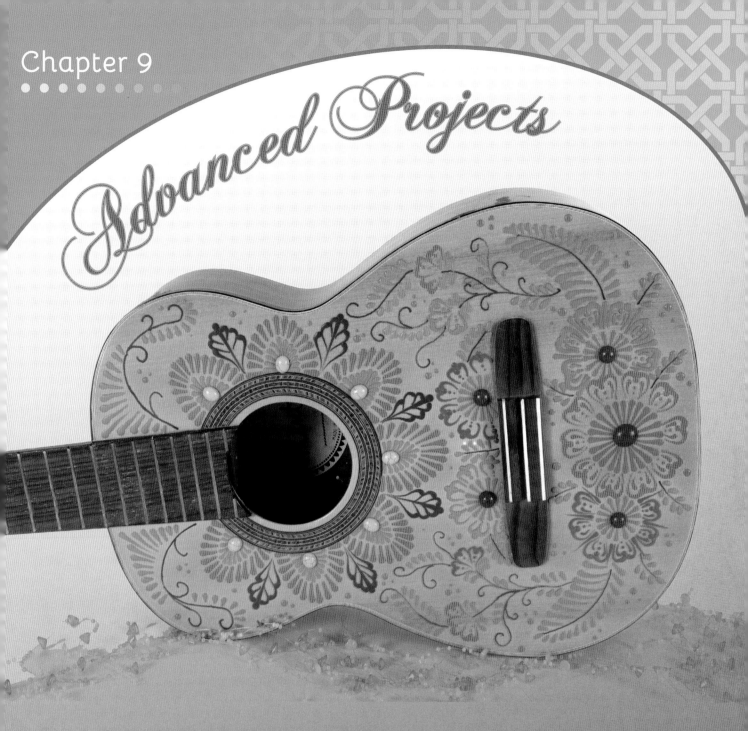

Secret Garden Guitar

1.

How many of you have an old guitar around, one that has been in the attic for years? Maybe it is beat up, warped, and does not really play anymore but you don't have the heart to get rid of it. If you don't already have one, check yard sales, thrift stores, or look on Craigslist. That's where I found mine.

2.

To prepare the guitar, I sanded it lightly with a very fine sanding disk to remove any scratches and to rough up the sealer just a little. Make sure your sandpaper is superfine; if you are scratching the guitar, your

sandpaper is not fine enough. Remove the strings, and always sand with the grain of the wood.

3.

This is one of the few times that I draw the complete pattern on the piece before I start the wax design. Start with the oval MJ Craft Templates. Select a template with a size that will work evenly in the space around the sound hole. With your white charcoal pencil, trace along about half of the oval template up to the design on the sound hole. By starting with the sound hole, you fill a lot of area and it is easier to decide what design and decoration you need in other areas. Place the next smaller oval template inside the first one, and trace along the inside of the smaller template to give you two half oval shapes.

4.

Move down to the bottom of the guitar below the bridge and pick the circle MJ Craft Template of the size you'd like for the flower that will be in the middle. Trace that line on. Move down one size from the template you just used and place it to the side of the center circle, overlapping it a bit. Starting near the top where the template meets the center circle's line, draw the line to create your smaller side circle; trace around the template until you meet up with the center circle line again at the bottom. Repeat on the left side to make the second side circle. Place smaller circles inside each flower to form their centers. Draw cosmos flower petals between the two lines of each circle.

Add fern-like leaves or a leaf of your choice in between the flowers. Add two larger leaves at the side edges of the flowers to fill in space. You do not have to draw the whole stroke as the photo shows; you can draw just the center line of the leaf, marking where you want it to go.

5.

Move to the area above the bridge. Draw two flowers here, coming out from the bridge: lay your circle template, starting with its larger outside circle, on part of the bridge. Then trace the portion of the circle

that lies on the body of the guitar. It should be about two-thirds of the circle. Find a circle size that you want for the center of these flowers and trace them the same way. Add leaves in between the flowers and outside the flowers.

6.

Now fill the open area on both sides, between the sound hole design and the bottom flowers, with a couple of half cosmos. The half cosmos are done in the same way as a cosmos, but with only three petals. Add two

or three of these half cosmos to each side as needed, to fill the areas. Put a couple of smaller fern leaves under them along with some wispy vine curls. Above each flower's petals, add a fern leaf.

7.

Add more drama by adding fern leaves to the top of the guitar on both sides to fill in the top area. Have two of the fern leaves going in one direction, with a good curl at the ends, and one going in the other direction.

8.

Look at your design and check whether you have filled in all of the open areas. Remember, although here we are drawing on the complete pattern, you may find it easier to draw the design onto one area at a time,

apply the wax design to it, and then move on to the next area. Do what works for you.

9.

I find it easier to start at the top of the guitar and work my way down. You may decide to do all the leaves at one time, then all the flowers, and so on; this also depends on how many melting pots you have, of course. You

can do this project with just one melting pot, completing all the work of one color before moving on to the next color.

Start with green in your melting pot. Place the MJ Wax Liner into the green wax in the melting pot to warm. Once the wax liner is warm, trace the veins of the fern leaves at the top of the guitar.

10.

Switch to yellow-green and, using a smaller wax tool for the smaller strokes and a larger wax tool for the larger strokes, put on the petals of the leaves. For the longer petals, you will pull the stroke longer. For the smaller petals you will pull and lift, to create a small stroke.

11.

With carnation pink and a medium tool, pull strokes from the outside oval line around the sound hole, to the inside oval line. Stop when you reach the line. By now you should have a pretty good idea of what size tool is best for the work.

12.

With your white charcoal pencil, mark a dot in the bottom center of each small oval to know where to pull your strokes to. Using robin's egg (or blue-green and white mixed half and half), start dividing the strokes off in the small oval. Pull the first stroke from the top of the oval until you run out of wax or reach the dot at the bottom. Next pull a stroke at the bottom of the oval, just above the sound hole design. Pull the stroke to the center on each side. Continue to divide the oval off until you have it filled.

13.

Put some heart leaves in between each of the petals using green. Measure out the same length at each meeting of the flower petal bases, and from that point pull a long stroke in until you run out of wax or

meet the petals. Pull at least three strokes on each side of the heart leaves. This will complete the top half of the guitar design.

14.

Next work on the cosmos flowers at the bottom. Using orange wax, you will create a circle design in the center of each flower (or you can always try another idea, like doing a center with dots instead). To

do the circle design, mark a dot in the center of the circle with your white charcoal pencil. Starting on the outside line of the circle, pull a stroke until you run out of wax or come to the dot. Choose a tool of the size that pulls the needed amount of wax for this. Now pull a stroke from the other side to divide the circle in half. Pull two more strokes to divide it in quarters. Continue to divide and add strokes until you have filled in the center of the flower. Use a smaller tool for the circles where the strokes go into the bridge.

15.

Using carnation pink, add the petals to the center cosmos. Add descending dots down the center of the petal and a small stroke on each side.

19.

Create the half cosmos flowers with any of the colors used for the others. Do the petals the same way. Add descending dots down the middle. If you have room for the strokes on the sides of the petals, add them.

16.

For the left side's cosmos, I mixed a little white wax with purple to lighten it. Create the petals on the cosmos to the left. Do the cosmos the same way as the middle one but add strokes in between the petals, 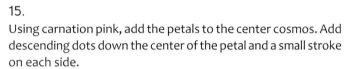 starting at the center and pulling the stroke until you run out of wax.

20.

Using the wax liner and green wax, add the veins for the fern leaves. (This should be all of the leaves remaining to do on the design.) Make sure to do a nice curl at the top of the leaves.

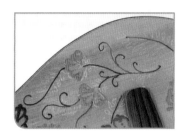

17.

With robin's egg, do a cosmos on the right side of the center flower. Do the flower the same as the middle flower, but pull the strokes that are in between the petals from the outside of the flower to the center. The  strokes should start at the same height as the petals do.

18.

Move on to the flowers above the bridge. Reverse the colors you used on the left and right flowers below. Add the petals and do descending dots down the middle. Add a dot to the top middle of the petals.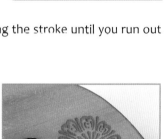

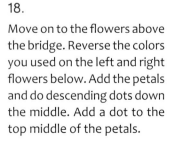

21.

Switching to yellow-green, add the individual petals to the leaves. Remember to use the right tool for the size of stroke you want.

22.

Now that you have completed your design, wipe the white charcoal lines off with a damp Magic Eraser. Gently rub the Magic Eraser with the direction of the wax strokes. Wipe the guitar off with a damp paper towel to remove the chalky film left by the Magic Eraser. Remove any fingerprints left on the guitar.

24.

Before sealing the top of the guitar with epoxy resin, I placed floral clay adhesive tape, which is waterproof, around the side of the guitar and around the sound hole to make a barrier. This protects the other parts of the guitar from any stray epoxy resin. Also, though epoxy resin is made to work over already-sealed items, manufacturers' ingredients do change. So I recommend first applying a test area of epoxy resin somewhere on the back of your guitar, just to play it safe.

Mix the resin per the manufacturer's instructions and pour it on top of the guitar. Make sure you have enough to cover the entire area. Spread the resin around with a wooden craft stick, making sure that it covers the wax completely, especially in areas where the wax is higher, like a dot, for example. Do not move the guitar while the resin is drying.

Once it is dry, remove the floral clay adhesive tape and sand the edges if needed to remove any remnants of it. Make sure you use a fine-grit sandpaper or sanding disk.

To clean up the centers of the flowers, glue on stones using permanent craft adhesive like E6000. If you plan to play the guitar, you might want to choose small flat stones. Let dry for twenty-four hours.

23.

Add descending dots in orange wax wherever you need just a little something more to fill an area. Use one or two dots where there is not enough room for three dots.

Things to Think About...

What if you did a sunflower around the sound hole? What leaves would you like better? What designs can you envision on a guitar? You might like more symmetrical designs, perhaps to match a different style of guitar. How about using metallic crayons in the design? What about an elegant design using swirls and fleurs-de-lis with pearls for embellishments?

Color Bubble Burst ●

On this project you are going to use lots of color. The key to making this an easier project is to just go with the flow and not overthink it. Start with a stretched canvas. Think about choosing a size that will fit into a ready-made frame, to complete the look of your finished picture.

Do a test stroke on the side or back of the canvas. If the stroke pulls a little rough, coat the front side of the canvas with gesso. I put two coats of gesso on my canvas until I got a smooth stroke. Let the gesso dry.

Use alcohol inks for this project. I used Adirondack® alcohol inks. You can find them in the scrapbooking section of craft stores or from vendors online. Do not use any of the metallic alcohol inks. They are thicker and will not spread out. Alcohol inks bleed out more than other inks, which is what you want in this project. Alcohol ink is fun to work with, and you can't mess it up.

You will be using isopropyl alcohol in a spray bottle to spray alcohol onto the canvas, which will make the alcohol ink spread even more.

1.

Start in a corner of the canvas and work your way in toward the middle. Spray the canvas with a squirt of alcohol. then put a couple drops of alcohol ink into that sprayed area. The bigger you want the colored area to be, the more ink you should drop on the canvas.

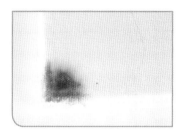

2.

Use a fan brush or a rake brush to pull the color out from the middle of the area. This walks the color out farther. Do not worry about the color not being as bright; you are going to add more color.

3.

I used lettuce green. Add a couple more drops in the same place you dropped the original color. This puts the brightness of color back into the design. If it bleeds enough, leave it. If you want it to bleed out a little more, squirt it with a bit of the alcohol. Just a little, not too much. You can always add more.

4.

Go to the next corner and apply your color the same way. The orange color I used is called sunset orange. Move on to the next corner.

5.

If you don't prefer the faded out look, try spraying the canvas with alcohol, adding the alcohol inks—maybe a couple colors at a time—and spraying it again with the alcohol. The color will not bleed as much and you will have brighter color, with a mottled look.

6.

Continue to add more colors to your canvas. Make sure to leave enough room between colors so that you can pull the color out. Blend each color into the edges of the last color. Don't these look like flowers? You could add wax on top of these to turn them into a bright flower patch.

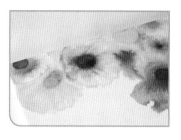

7.

Don't worry if you accidentally drop a stray bit of alcohol ink. Just go with it. See? You really can't mess up! For any blank sections that remain to fill in, wet the area with alcohol and add a little alcohol ink into that section. Leave it muted; do not pull the color out.

Some of the colors I used were butterscotch, purple twilight, orange sunset, red pepper, eggplant, and stream. Do not get stuck thinking only in my colors!

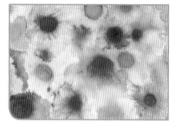

8.

Heat set the alcohol ink with an embossing tool. (This step has to be done before you apply the wax, which would melt when heated.) Heat a section at a time for 30 seconds. This keeps the color from bleeding when spray varnish is applied, and also dries any parts of the canvas that may be wet from the alcohol and the inks.

9.

Spray the canvas with a spray varnish. Make sure that it is a non-yellowing varnish. Krylon makes a varnish that is specifically for canvas. Let the varnish dry. This coat keeps the canvas clean and also helps the white charcoal pencil to show up better, and remove more easily.

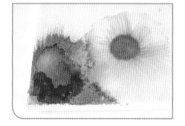

10.

Starting again at the corner, use the circle MJ Craft Templates to draw the circles on the canvas with white charcoal pencil. I started with a double circle using two templates one inside of the other, tracing on the inside of each template.

11.

You want all sizes of circles, and a variety of single circles, double circles, and triple circles. Use a large circle template and put it more than halfway on from the edge of the canvas. Trace along the inside of the circle with your white charcoal pencil.

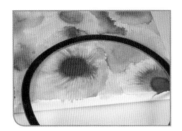

12.

Add two more circle templates and trace them with your pencil. Add another two more templates and trace again. This gives you fatter circles inside of each other.

13.

Continue to add circles to the canvas, with circles underneath other circles.

14.

Draw half circles or some that are just a little over half a circle. A larger fraction than that can be hard to apply the wax to. Try not to make all the same size circles next to each other—mix it up. Have fun...there is no right or wrong.

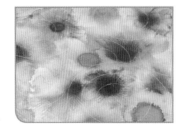

15.

Use the circle Mini MJ Craft Templates to make smaller circles in between the larger ones. Fill in all the circle-free areas.

16.

Pick crayons that go with the colors on the canvas. Lay them onto your canvas to see how they complement the rest of the colors. I used red, orange, dandelion, yellow-green, cerulean, and purple. I also used a little white to lighten colors of the darker blue and purple crayons.

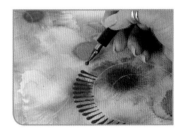

17.

Start with a wax color that matches a color inside the circle you are working on. Use a size of tool that's appropriate for the area. Pull the stroke from the outside line to the inside line. Do strokes next to each other when working in a large circle. (You could divide the circle off but it would be a little more difficult, and might not end up as evenly spaced.) Try to keep the strokes the same distance apart. If you are right handed, work to the right around the circle.

18.

To get just the tails of a stroke onto the canvas, place a piece of paper next to the canvas and pull the stroke starting on the paper, with the thin tail ending up on the canvas. This gives you the correct size of tail, making the circle look correct.

19.

Create a circle within a circle. Start at the second circle's line and pull in until you reach the third circle. You can leave the design like this. or you can do a circle design in the center circle too. Remember to carry

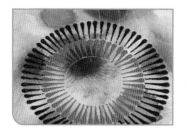

your tool loaded with wax around the canvas, not over the canvas, to where you are applying your stroke so that if the wax drips it doesn't land on the canvas.

20.

If you are working on a smaller circle, divide the circle into sections and keep dividing. Notice the circle portion here; as mentioned earlier, if you include larger-than-half circles in your design, you could have problems adding the strokes correctly.

21.

Start at the second circle and pull a stroke in between the dandelion strokes. Pull the stroke until it runs out of wax or you reach the center of the inside circle. With yellow-green, starting just above the dande-

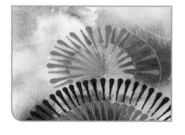

lion strokes, pull the stroke out until you reach the outside line.

22.

Do some circles with just a single row of wax. The larger open circle makes it more dramatic. Mix up the designs. Try not to have two of the same design next to each other.

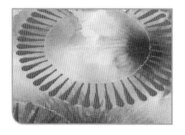

23.

Do a double circle and pull a stroke starting at the outside circle in between the red strokes, stopping just above the dandelion strokes. This is the opposite of the half circle you did last time. Do a whole

circle instead of a half. Add a dot to clean up the middle.

24.

This design looks like a bubble popping! Start with three circles. Make sure the circle in the middle is not too small. Start by doing a circle design beginning at the second circle and pulling it until it runs out

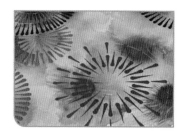

of wax. Divide the circle off. Leave enough room for another set of strokes in between. Pull the second set of strokes outward starting at the center circle. Pull the strokes until they run out of wax. Pull the last set of strokes starting at the outside circle and pull just above the strokes that are pulled to the center of the circle.

25.

For a larger circle with three sets of circles, start on the inside of the second circle and pull toward the center until you reach the first circle. Switch to the other ends of the strokes, pull a set of strokes

out starting above each stroke you just did. You can stop at the line if you like, or you can pull the stroke until it runs out. If you are loading your melting pot correctly and not letting it get too low on wax, the strokes will all end up being the same length. Put a very small circle in the center. Pull the strokes outward until they run out of wax. The strokes can touch each other on the center circle. Add a dot to clean up the center.

26.

This design is made with three circles from the circle Mini MJ Craft Templates. Start on the outside circle and pull a dandelion stroke to the middle or until it runs out of wax. Divide the circle into eight strokes. Then, using red, do a

stroke on each side of the dandelion strokes starting at the second line, for a total of sixteen strokes. Keep the strokes spaced far enough to leave room for one more stroke. With purple, start the last stroke at the top of the inside circle and pull to the middle. There will be a total of eight strokes between the red strokes. Add a dot to clean up the center.

27.

Do some circles with three rows of strokes not overlapping. In small areas, use a design of just one circle. Add a dot to the centers of circles as needed.

28.

With a damp paper towel, gently rub off the white charcoal pencil marks. Rub in the direction of the strokes; do not work against the strokes. Let the canvas dry.

29.

Spray the canvas again with spray varnish. This brings the shine back to the wax. All artwork should be kept out of direct sunlight. The wax will melt if placed in direct sun, because there's no heavy varnish on the canvas.

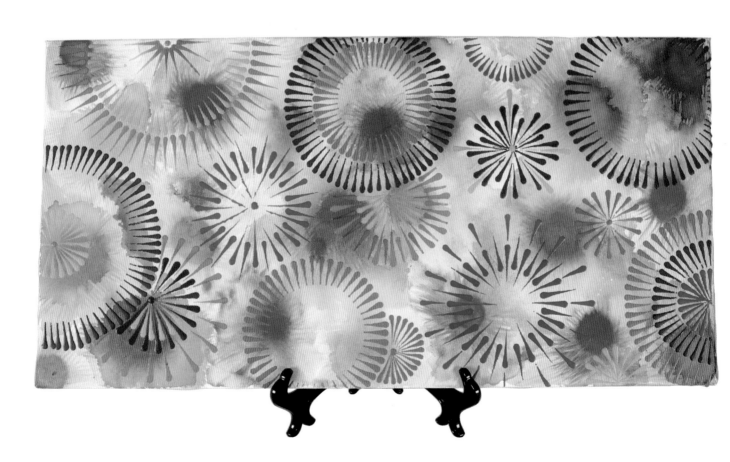

Conclusion

The goal of *Wax on Crafts* is to get you thinking of ways you can add wax to simple and inexpensive items that you see every day. We've walked step by step through all sorts of uses for wax design, starting with simple projects and adding more great ideas as we went.

Now that you have the basics down, you can complete any of these projects in hours—some even in minutes. The hardest part of the process is, simply, not to overthink it. Don't make wax decorating harder than it is; just relax and have fun. Once you are having fun, watch out, because you won't want to stop! If you get those creative juices flowing with ideas, you will be amazed at all the projects and designs you will come up with. Enjoy.

Should you need to contact me, please email me at **Art@miriamjoy.com**. I make every effort to return your email within twenty-four hours of receiving it.

I can be reached through the social media websites listed below:

Facebook: **Miriam Joy's Waxy Crafty Corner**
Facebook: **Miriam Joy Gourd Creations**
Pinterest: **www.pinterest.com/miriamjoysagen**
YouTube: **www.youtube.com/user/Miriamjoy123**

Thank you for purchasing this book and supporting my artistic ideas and products.

God bless,
Miriam Joy

Miriam Joy's Products and Supplies

I invite you take time visit the MJ products that I have featured in this book. I am constantly updating this page with new and innovative products for you to enjoy. The website with featured products can be found at **www.miriamjoy.com.**

I am constantly working on new projects and new YouTube videos for you. You can subscribe to my YouTube channel so that you can get all the latest videos on YouTube at Miriamjoy123 or type in the direct link **https://www.youtube.com/user/Miriamjoy123.**

I also have a Facebook page at "Miriam Joy's Waxy Crafty Corner." I post pictures of projects and other craft items on this page for you to make and be inspired.

For your convenience I offer Paypal or any major credit card should you wish to purchase products from my website.